ZEST

Your Life

A Taste of Inner Wisdom

A Taste of Inner Wisdom

Linda Babulic

LEADERS IN GLOBAL PUBLISHING

Published by Motivational Press, Inc.
1777 Aurora Road
Melbourne, Florida, 32935
www.MotivationalPress.com

Copyright 2015 © by Linda Babulic

All Rights Reserved

No part of this book may be reproduced or transmitted in any form by any means: graphic, electronic, or mechanical, including photocopying, recording, taping or by any information storage or retrieval system without permission, in writing, from the authors, except for the inclusion of brief quotations in a review, article, book, or academic paper. The authors and publisher of this book and the associated materials have used their best efforts in preparing this material. The authors and publisher make no representations or warranties with respect to accuracy, applicability, fitness or completeness of the contents of this material. They disclaim any warranties expressed or implied, merchantability, or fitness for any particular purpose. The authors and publisher shall in no event be held liable for any loss or other damages, including but not limited to special, incidental, consequential, or other damages. If you have any questions or concerns, the advice of a competent professional should be sought.

In selected anecdotes in this book, names and identifying characteristics have been changed to protect the privacy of the individuals.

Manufactured in the United States of America.

ISBN: 978-1-62865-220-8

Dedication

As a facilitator, coach, and speaker, I have had the
privilege of seeing women recognize and uncover their
inner strength and beauty—thereby transforming
their lives. They proved and validated that the material
and information that I share in this book works with
fast, proven results. I'd like to thank them for sharing
their journeys with me and providing their stories of
challenge, courage, and triumph. They have all found
ZEST in their own ways. Thank you.

I dedicate this book to my husband Jon, my family, and
my friends. You have supported me through numerous
and sometimes crazy ideas and adventures. It's because
of you that I have a ZESTY fun-filled life. Thank you.

Contents

ZEST Your Life - A Taste of Inner Wisdom 11

Introduction: What is ZEST? 13

How to Work with This Book.. 16

PART 1: AWAKEN THE WOMAN WITHIN 16

PART 2: CREATE EMOTIONAL MATURITY......................... 17

PART 3: CONNECT MIND & BODY................................ 18

PART 4: LIVE YOUR ZEST 18

PART 1
AWAKEN THE WOMAN WITHIN

Chapter 1 Your Inner Power!....................................**24**

The Seven Secrets of Women with ZEST 24

Awaken Your Power 26

Where Power Resides... 26

Why the Womb? 27

Measuring Your Womb Power 29

Qualities of a Powerful Woman 30

Your Power-Filled Stories 32

Accessing Your Power-Filled Stories 33

Relationships 36

The Lake Meditation—15 Minutes 40

The People You Spend the Most Time With 44

Council of Wise Women 46

Chapter 2 Finding Authenticity **49**

Who Has Your Power? 50

Your Ideal Life 53

Chapter 3 Communication **55**

Active Listening 57

Understanding 61

The Inconsistent Message 62

Questions 64

Time and Place 68

Lies 68

Intuition 69

Barriers to Effective Communication 70

Communicate for ZEST 71

Chapter 4 Part 1 ZESTERS **73**

Call to Action 74

PART 2
CREATE EMOTIONAL MATURITY

Chapter 5 Emotions **78**

What Are Emotions? 78

Be Aware and In Tune with How You Feel 79

Emotional Reactions to Physical Changes 81

Emotionally Discerning Communication 83

Emotional Authenticity 84

Emotionally Grounded 85

Where You Put Your Energy 85

Circle of Concern and Circle of Influence 86

Circles: What Goes Where? 87

Objects 88

Environment 90

Money 91

The Emotional Bank Account 92

Deposits and Withdrawals 93

Deposits for Life 94

Chapter 6 Barriers to Emotional ZEST 96

Emotionality 96

Fear 98

Examples of Limiting Fears: 101

Feeling and Behaving Like a Victim 103

Anger 105

Guilt 106

Words 107

I Am/I Should 107

Chapter 7 Emotional Masks 109

Mask Dance 111

Masks Show and Tell 112

Masks Built on Beliefs 114

Remove the Masks 117

Your Greatest Mask 118

Chapter 8 Applying the Change 121

Your Gifts 122

Storytelling 123

Create Emotional Maturity Review 125

Emotionally Discerning Communication 126

Emotionally Authentic 126

Emotionally Grounded 126

Standing Strong in Your Power-filled ZEST Stories 127

Chapter 9 Part 2 ZESTERS 128

The World's Most Unusual Therapist by Dr. Joe Vitale 129

Call to Action 134

PART 3
CONNECT MIND/BODY

Chapter 10 Mind/Body Research.. **136**

    The "Feel Good" Hormone.. 137

    Creating Uplifting Emotions 138

    Visualization.. 139

    The Mind/Body Well-Being Checklist 139

Chapter 11 Mind/Mental Aspect **143**

    States of Conscious and Levels of Awareness.................... 144

    Fear 146

    Mental Health 147

Chapter 12 The Body... **149**

    Bone Density.. 149

    Chakras 150

    Note the Seven Major Chakras 151

    Universal Life Force Energy 155

Chapter 13 Barriers to Body ZEST **156**

    Heart Disease 156

    Thyroid 157

    Cancer.. 157

    Immune System.. 157

    Aging.. 158

    Beliefs and Trauma 159

    Money.. 160

Chapter 14 Mind/Body Working Together **161**

    Mind/Body Connection to Disease.................................... 162

    Personal Appearance and Image... 162

Chapter 15 Barriers to Mind/Body ZEST 165

Junk Food 165

Toxic Thoughts Are Junk Food for the Mind 165

Complaining 166

Chapter 16 Part 3 ZESTERS 168

ZEST Stones 173

Breathe 174

Call to Action 175

PART 4
LIVE YOUR ZEST!

Chapter 17 What is Spiritual ZEST? 179

Feel Spiritual ZEST 180

Chapter 18 Barriers to Spiritual ZEST 184

Chapter 19 Spiritual/Sensual Connection 186

Chapter 20 Align Your Feelings and Beliefs 188

Satisfaction, Frustration, and Desires 189

Clarification 189

Chapter 21 Values: Maps that Guide You 191

All I Really Need To Know I Learned in Kindergarten 192

Clarify and Prioritize Your Current Values—Part One 193

Values in Action—Part Two 196

Chapter 22 Freedom 199

Chapter 23 Your Authentic Self 201

Be Who You Really Are 201

Positive Power Talk 203

Passion Power 204

Chapter 24 Create a ZEST Vision Board..................................209

Chapter 25 Tests and Challenges 215
    Catalyst 217
    Live Your ZEST Review 217

Chapter 26 Part 4—ZESTERS....................................219
    Blessed Beauty Way Prayer...223

Chapter 27 Why Now?..227
    It's the Best Time to Be a Woman! 228
    Love Your Life 229
    Your Act of Power..231

About the Author..233
Recommended Resources..234
References 236

ZEST Your Life -
A Taste of Inner Wisdom

Foreword by Justin Sachs

Congratulations on your decision to step up, and take it to the next level to design the life you desire. It's well known that building relationships are crucial to success. And that trust is of paramount importance in every relationship. The first and most important relationship you must build is with yourself and you must trust yourself. *ZEST Your Life - A Taste of Inner Wisdom* will gently nudge you in the right direction to find the person you are meant to be and life you are destined to have.

All over the world, I am meeting people who have lost connection to themselves, their friends, family, and their community. They don't believe that change is possible for them. They have forgotten their own dreams, desires and goals while they were helping everyone get what they want. They have forgotten that it is their right and their destiny to be joyous, vibrant and happy. Has this happened to you? It happened to me. We get so busy with our lives that we can forget about ourselves. When this is happening we need to rebuild our relationship with our authentic self, the powerful, ZESTY person who radiates joy, vibrancy and happiness.

The media abounds with stories of challenges met, changes effected and success achieved. It's time to awaken the woman within, to convene the support of a Council of Wise Women and to hone the effective communications skills to build strong relationships. You can learn to gain emotional maturity and deal with situations as they arise and from the maturity that you have now, not from a place of pain and victimization. You can monitor the emotional reactions to physical changes and understand where, when and how to use, share and dispense your energy. The mind/body research links healing responses with mental and emotional changes. States of consciousness and levels of mental awareness are cornerstones to understanding yourself and others.

You too can Zero-in and focus on what you want your life to be, get Excited to have a life that you love, achieve Success in any way you define it and Transcend to a higher level of living the life you are meant to have.

When you work through the exercises, implement the *ZESTERS* (thing you do and action you take to activate the ZEST in your life) you will be shocked at how easily you uncover a clear vision of the life you want, make decisions and take action to have the life you are longing for. Every joy, sorrow and challenge you have experienced in your life have led you to this moment, to this page and to make the choice to have what you want.

I challenge you to apply the power of persistence and make the most of the *Seven Secrets of Women with ZEST.* They:

1. *Stand strong in their personal power*
2. *Don't let fear stop them*
3. *Consciously direct their thoughts and feelings*
4. *Manage their time and agendas*
5. *Honor their dreams and desires*
6. *Take action to make a difference*
7. *Love their lives*

Introduction: What is ZEST?

Now is the time to take your life up a notch or two, from what it is to what it could be—which is *so much more*. Don't you want to find a comforting place; one with harmony and balance? Discover more about yourself and how to explore and expand your joy, passion, and enthusiasm. That process of discovery involves creating freedom, inner power, and self-responsibility.

For a moment, let's imagine a life filled with ZEST. You Zero-in and focus on exactly what you want in your life, what you want your life to look and feel like for your greater good. You have the enthusiasm to get out of bed and you Expect to make a difference in the world. Expect the best and it happens. When you give, you also receive. You soar to bigger dreams and successes than your mind can currently conceive. Achieve Success in the emotional, physical, mental, and spiritual aspects—you define it for yourself. As you increase your connections to your higher self and your higher calling, you Transcend to a place of joy, peace, and vibrancy. You don't just survive, you thrive. Let's review:

ZEST=

Zero-in

Expect

Success

Transcend

"By transcending to your personal core, the higher self,
you discover your true nature—a blissful self of infinite worth.
It [the higher self] is the 'you' behind all of the defenses and images you
have created for yourself…
the you that really knows why you are here,
what it is you need, and how you can get it."
—Dr. Deepak Chopra

ZEST is a feeling. It's the passion that moves you forward. It gets you out of bed in the morning, eager to accomplish, achieve your dreams, and focus on your desires. It's the fire in your belly. It's that magic and mystery that caused you to progress from riding a tricycle, to riding a bicycle, to driving a car. You never questioned whether you should stop riding your tricycle, did you? Naturally, you just took the next step. You had no doubts about it. You were living your ZEST.

Learn the process necessary to support change, ignite your inner fire, and gain control of your challenges—like the women who have experienced the fast, proven results of the *ZEST Your Life* programs. In December 2011, I facilitated the first *ZEST Your Life* programs. They offered women a special opportunity to learn, explore, and experience what many described as a life changing understanding of what mattered most to them. Participants engaged in experiential activities, shared their stories, and were gently supported to go deep within and uncover their true dreams and desires. To learn more about these programs, go to www.ZESTyourLife.com.

The online *British English Thesaurus* says:

Zest originally denoted the grated outer rind of a lemon, orange, or lime; hence it has also come to refer to a quality of excitement or piquancy. For example: *I try to beat previous records in order to give* zest *to an otherwise monotonous job.* It also describes the eager enthusiasm inspired by such a quality. For example: *The grass court season has given him renewed zest, and he is playing the best tennis of his career,* or *She had a* zest *for life and boundless energy.*

Here are some synonyms for ZEST: enthusiasm, gusto, relish, appetite, eagerness, keenness, avidity, zeal, fervor, ardor, passion, love, enjoyment, joy, delight, excitement, verve, vigor, liveliness, sparkle, fizz, effervescence, fire, animation, vitality, dynamism, energy, buoyancy, brio, bounce, pep, spirit, exuberance, high spirits, informal zing, zip, oomph, vim, pizzazz, get-up-and-go.

I use these terms and phrases throughout the book to help you create your own understanding of the feeling that is ZEST. I also asked women on the Facebook group page: www.Facebook.com/groups/zestyourlife to complete the following sentence: *A ZESTY woman is...* Here's what they said:

- Valerie Leonard — *...sure to add zing to any situation. I strive to have ZESTY zing in everything I do! Cheers to all the ZESTY women out there!*

- Pat Durant—*...full of love, respectful of others, and reaches for the stars!*

- Carol Hume—*...free to be her authentic self and not what everyone else wants her to be.*

- Jill Ellis—*...strong and confident, with a great sense of humor!*

- Deborah MacDonald—*...passionate, on purpose and kick-ass for fun and freedom!*

- Diana Lidstone—*The more that a zesty woman can shine brightly, the more she can share her unique gifts with so many others!*

- Carol-Chantal Séguin—*...ambitious, brilliant, courageous, diligent, excited, fearless...all the way to z... ZESTY!*

- Dana Pharant—*...one who lives with no excuses and no apologies, head held high and having a blast!*

- Julie Poirier—...*a woman who does everything with heart and soul and exudes a certain amount of "je ne sais quoi"...A ZESTY Disposition!!*

How to Work with This Book

You can read the book and do the exercises on your own, but the process is even more effective and powerful when you gather a few women and go through the book together. An energy and vibration frequency attracts women to share their lives and stories. You may feel this vibration when you speak with other women, knowing that they are also eager to improve their lives. You know that you are not alone. You also feel this energy as you prepare a place in your schedule and heart to awaken the woman within.

Women gather for many different reasons: building a playground, saving a hospital or school from closing, joining a book club, creating a play group, engaging in an exercise class, or simply to be with each other. When women gather an *energy dome* is created. Whatever is created in this energy dome is strong and enduring because of their intent.

Part of the overall intent should be to honor the beauty, strength, and vitality of women. Doing so inspires, motivates, and provides women with the courage to try something new or finally make a dream become reality. Sometimes the new dreams that are born are disconnected from the original reason that pulled these women together. You never know what could happen when you open your heart.

The book is divided into four parts to help navigate the process of uncovering, activating, and unleashing your ZEST:

PART 1: AWAKEN THE WOMAN WITHIN

- Awaken your inner spirit and take action to improve your life.

- Access the *Seven Secrets of Women with ZEST* that are throughout the book.

- Explore questions and exercises to awaken power; find where it resides and how it feels.

- Identify the qualities and stories you have in common with other powerful women.

- Discover the emotional impact and influence connected to your immediate relationships.

- Convene your personal Council of Wise Women.

- Find your authentic self to design, develop, and live your ideal life.

- Cultivate your active listening skills, gain understanding by asking questions, and open your heart to be aware and awake during all of your communications with yourself and others.

- Upgrade your intuition, inner guidance, and external communications.

PART 2: CREATE EMOTIONAL MATURITY

- Embrace that you are complex, intricate, and elaborate.

- Be aware and in tune with how you feel.

- Monitor emotional reactions to physical changes.

- Practice discerning communication that is emotionally authentic and grounded.

- Clearly understand where, when, and how to use, share, and dispense your energy.

- Dissolve the barriers of emotionality, fear, anger, and guilt.

- Learn to speak the words of reconciliation and forgiveness.

- Remove the emotional masks built on false beliefs and thought patterns.

- Implement ZESTERS—the things you do and actions you take to activate ZEST in your life.

PART 3: CONNECT MIND & BODY

- Learn the research that links healing responses with mental and emotional changes.

- Release the "feel good" hormone and create uplifting emotions.

- Score yourself on the mind/body well-being checklist.

- Explore states of consciousness and levels of mental awareness.

- Discover the science behind building bone density.

- Connect to your chakras and the universal life-force energy.

- Uncover how you think, feel, and express yourself and discover the energetic effect on your physical body.

- Link with Mother Earth through her "stone" gifts.

PART 4: LIVE YOUR ZEST

- Intend and manifest that this year and beyond will become the best years of your life.

- Answer the call of inner knowing.

- Spirituality allows for the possibility that our desires will manifest, our dreams will come true, and the unexplainable will happen.

- Find the Goddess that resonates in you.

- Manifest the spiritual/sensual connection to your higher self.

- Align your feelings and beliefs to gain clarity.

- Clarify and prioritize your current values and put them into action on a vision board.

- Implement vibrant freedom in each aspect: emotional, physical, mental, and spiritual.

Each chapter includes special features to help you easily process the information and apply it to your life. There are powerful quotes, definitions, contextual substance, exercises, take-aways, and affirmations anchor the learning from each exercise.

The exercises may seem inconsequential while you are doing them, but the result is a subtle paradigm shift allowing you to hold a vision of yourself that is positive, uplifting, and empowering. To make it easy to take notes and track the progress you are making towards your dreams and desires, download the exercise workbook at www.ZESTyourLife. com/extras.

The affirmations throughout the book concisely summarize the information presented and focus your intention on applying it. As you reflect on these truths, this wisdom becomes so integrated into your thinking and mindset that you won't remember a time when you did not feel fully awake, aware, and awesome.

Each part of the book closes with ZESTERS, which are the things you do and actions you take to activate the ZEST in your life. For a printable list of ZESTERS go to www.ZESTyourLife.com/extras.

The information in this book is intended to provide comfort and healing. Take care of yourself as you read it, and take a break if needed. You are the guiding light for what happens in your life. Take one step at a time on the path to your authentic, true self.

SuccZESTfully yours,
Linda

PART 1

AWAKEN THE WOMAN WITHIN

"Once the soul awakens, the search begins and you can never go back."
—*John O'Donohue*

You want to awaken your inner spirit and take action to improve your life. Maybe your inner fire has dimmed or gone out? Imagine your inner fire burning brightly. Imagine you are happy, your body feels strong and healthy, your mind is sharp, and your spirit is soaring.

I know that you want *more*: more balance, more peace, and more control of your time and energy. And I know that you want *less*: less ups and downs, less stress, and less unmanageable outside demands.

You may feel that your life is secure, stable and good enough. Yet you want, crave, and need to feed your soul and your *inner fire*. You yearn for the joy, passion, and satisfaction that you can only have when you live your life to the fullest, and when you seek to fulfill exciting dreams.

You know you deserve more vitality in your life. You know how great it feels. Taking care of your dreams and desires is not selfish. It's a necessary part of living a full life. When you live a zesty, joyful, and happy life everyone around you benefits. You're making the world a better place.

Can you awaken to the possibility that there is a more powerful, exciting, and impressive person inside you? You are being called to awaken the invisible power that has been taking a nap. When you buy a white car, suddenly you see white cars everywhere. Once you awaken your ZEST, you'll start to see ZEST everywhere.

When you have ZEST, you are the child on the bike. You feel the wind in your hair, you are free, and you hold your own inner power and strength. ZEST is the catalyst—the spark that holds and fuses the energies of your emotional, physical, mental, and spiritual aspects. Your energies become best friends holding hands.

The quality of your life is held in your dreams—the ones you have attained and the ones you have yet to actualize. To get the most out of your life, you must have a dream in your heart—a hope, an ambition that you want to realize, something that you want to attain, achieve, or complete. To accomplish this dream, you need to access the power, *your* power, that is held in your thoughts and beliefs about yourself. You need your dreams so that you can fulfill your promise...

> *"...our dreams as humans are not accidental, they are not random.*
> *They are our soul's means of reminding us what we are*
> *here to do to fulfill our promise..."*
> —*Kathleen McGowan*

To find those dreams, you may have to do a little digging...

A boy was given a pile of horse manure for his birthday. Immediately, he started digging, and all the while he kept smiling. Finally, someone asked him, "What are you doing?"

"With all this manure," the boy replied enthusiastically, digging away, "there's got to be a pony in here somewhere."

This boy had a dream to have a pony. Are you prepared to do what this boy did? Will you do a little dirty digging? Can you own your dream and the life that you want?

How does your life make you feel? Take a moment to think about your life: your significant relationships, your friends, your hobbies, your habits, your economic situation, your home, your car, your job. Do you have the courage to create the life you want in all these areas?

Nap time is over. Let's awaken the woman inside of you. We'll unlock the energies of your personal power, explore the barriers that hold you back, and create a path to find and liberate your authentic life and dreams.

"Our dreams are extensions of ourselves. In order to live a dream-come-true life, you have to invest time and effort in learning about yourself."
—Marcia Wieder

Chapter 1
Your Inner Power!

Have you ever wondered why some women look so fabulous? They're happy, they're vibrant, and they're ZESTY. You try to guess how old they are, but you guess them to be years younger than their actual age. Wouldn't it be great if you knew how they did it? Read on to access their secrets and how you can have them.

The Seven Secrets of Women with ZEST

They:

1. Stand strong in their personal power.

2. Don't let fear stop them.

3. Consciously direct their thoughts and feelings.

4. Manage their time and agendas.

5. Honor their dreams and desires.

6. Take action to make a difference.

7. Love their lives.

You are a powerful woman, but before you use your power, you must rediscover and awaken your power. Get to know your power intimately—how it feels, what makes it big, and what makes it small—because the size matters.

When I commuted to work, I did an experiment. I wanted to see the measure of my power and if I could have a positive impact. One morning, when I was on the bus, I sat next to the window. During the forty minute ride, several people sat next to me. To each new person, I said, "Good morning," with a big smile. Every one of them sat a little straighter and they gave me a smile and a friendly "good morning."

The person I remember most vividly was a woman who was probably in her seventies. She sat next to me. I smiled and said: "Good morning." She nodded and smiled, but said nothing. She put her head down, seeming a bit shy. But when she was ready to exit the bus, she looked at me, and with tremendous effort and a thick accent, she stuttered: "Gud mornink."

In that moment, it was obvious that she had been rehearsing and getting the courage to respond to me. We shared a heart-to-heart connection; there was an exchange of energy and there was positive impact. I was encouraged that I could do something so simple, and yet have such a big impact and influence. That was a pretty good result for a smile and a "good morning."

Doing one little thing can make a big difference in someone's life. You have a greater influence than you might think. As you walk around a shopping mall, watch how people behave and the impact they have on you and others. Some are obviously distressed and disturbed—we walk around them. A baby crying or child having a meltdown turns heads. People who are laughing have an impact too.

Try this: walk through a shopping mall with your powerful heart fully open, a smile on your face, and your body standing tall. Watch the responses from the people around you.

Now try this, if you can. Walk through the shopping mall again, and make yourself energetically small and closed. Shake your head, mumble, and watch the responses you get.

Your power is contagious. How you put your power out into the world matters. It may be invisible, but its impact is not. Can you be more authentic and show more of the real you in the world? Can you be more loving, compassionate, and caring for yourself and others? Write down any thoughts and feelings as you go through this process to discover more about yourself. Take your time.

Awaken Your Power

Think about how you feel in your power right now at this moment, and complete the following sentence: My power feels_____. Then ask yourself:

What makes it big?

What makes it small?

Have you become aware of the size, impact, and influence that your powerful energy can have on those around you?

If you are not paying full attention to your life and consciously deciding where and how you want it to go, you'll soon be blown around like a leaf in the wind. Everyone else will be in control of your life and you will be left feeling listless and remorseful for the life you could have had.

Affirmation:
My power is contagious.
How I put my power into the world matters.

Where Power Resides

Author Lynn V. Andrews says, "For power to come to you, you must make a place within yourself for that power to live." For many women, me included, that place is the womb space.

We are all born from a mother's womb, and we each have a womb space. You may be interested to know that for men, it is the place from which they access feminine strength and beauty without aggressive action. For women, it is the place for our power to live. Your womb connects you to your mother, your grandmother, your great-grandmother, your great-great grandmother, etc. It is an unbroken lineage to the divine feminine energy. Not surprisingly, it is often called the Holy Womb.

Your womb's sole purpose is to nurture, grow, and create new life, even if you never give birth to a child. There is no better place to let go of the past, rebirth your own life, and to manifest the power, beauty, and abundance of joy that you desire.

In ancient times, the womb and childbearing were viewed as a source of mystery and magic. Today, there is no doubt that those assumptions were right. We can now witness the journey from conception to birth in 3D photos and HD videos, and in a way it certainly is mysterious and magical.

The claims of what the womb can do have extended beyond the physical life giving process. Although I didn't uncover any scientific proof, there is a great deal of support that could lead you to believe that it can do so much more. Having said that, I have a hard time arguing with Barbara Ma-El, founder of the *Way of the Womb* website, who recently shared: "Way of the Womb! (WoW) supports the healing and awakening of the feminine to give her deepest gift of love. When she gives this, the masculine is re-birthed into his nobility..."

WHY THE WOMB?

It is the fountain of perpetual joy, timeless wisdom, and sensuality.

It is an infinite wellspring of vitality, healing, and replenishment.

It calls forth the purity of a man's heart.

It gives man his second birth; a spiritual birth.

It is the foundation for the ceaseless flowering of a woman's heart.

It gives woman sanctuary, a safe place, eternally pure and inviolate.

It transmutes suffering and pain; patterns that do not serve life.

It transmutes distortions in DNA and activates latent DNA.

It dissolves all fear, returning everything to the innocence of love.

It births the soul's desire.

It breathes with eternity.

It gives life and absolves death.

... some call it "The Holy Grail."

www.WayOfTheWomb.com

Your power resides in your womb space. It is nearly impossible to understand that at almost the same moment the womb suffers, it is also begins healing itself immediately from those experiences. The womb feels everything a woman does: abuse, miscarriage, abortion, hysterectomy, negative sexuality, sexual attacks, heartbreaks, violence, and more. We become stronger through experience.

Uniting with our womb power shakes loose the old patterns of behavior. The more connected we are to our womb power, the more our cells literally shake at a higher vibrational frequency (faster and more often) and dissolve the armor that we build up. Think of this process as an earthquake shaking a bridge until it crumbles.

Creativity, intuition, and wisdom are seeded in the womb, germinate in the heart, then move to the mind to come to fruition. Awakening and engaging womb energy brings you in alignment with the divine feminine. The womb power becomes a source of never ending strength and resilience.

*"There is something beautiful about all scars of
whatever nature.*

*A scar means the hurt is over, the wound is closed
and healed, done with."*

—Harry Crews

MEASURING YOUR WOMB POWER

Let's look at your measure of womb power and how it lives in you—in your emotional, physical, mental, and spiritual energies. Put your hand on your womb space and take a few deep, cleansing breaths in and out to instantly reestablish your conscious connection to your inner strength and highest potential.

- Emotional. How do you feel emotionally when you are focusing on your womb and its power? Are you feeling clear, balanced, and capable? Do you remember a time when you felt the full extent of your power? Does looking back cause you to well up in tears? What emotion is attached to them?

- Physical body. How do you feel physically when you are connected to your womb power? Do you feel strong, healthy, and fully aware of your physicality? Is this different from how you normally feel? Do you get out of bed filled with energy? How do you feel when you go to bed?

- Mental. How do you feel mentally when you are focusing on your womb and its power? Are you feeling alert, conscious, and powerful? Do you make the best use of the mental gifts that you have?

- Spiritual. This term has various definitions or interpretations. A common meaning found in online dictionaries is "devotion to metaphysical matters, as opposed to worldly things". Another is "activities that renew, lift you up, comfort, heal, and inspire both yourself and those with whom you interact". In whatever way you define spirituality, is it something that feeds you? Are you feeling connected, uplifted, and supported? Are you following a spiritual practice, an attitude of gratitude? Do you have a connection to your higher self?

True power has nothing to do with being a public figure or how much money you have. True power is not ego driven, and it is not about having power over something or someone. Many people have failed because they abused their positions and let their self-important egos lead them to make bad decisions. Ego gives attachment to something falsely identified as power.

> *"Half of the harm that is done, in this world, is*
> *due to people who want to feel important.*
> *They don't mean to do harm, but the harm does*
> *not interest them."*
>
> —*T.S. Eliot*

QUALITIES OF A POWERFUL WOMAN

When you think of powerful women, who comes to mind? Your mom, your sister, your best friend, Oprah, Madonna, Lady Gaga?

How would you describe this woman or the women you are thinking about?

What strengths did they use to accomplish their successes?

What are the qualities of a powerful woman?

Take a moment to think about these questions and/or brainstorm. Write down the qualities of each woman. What qualities do they have in common? Are they:

- Love
- Balance
- Supportiveness
- Artistic nature
- Approachability
- Eagerness to learn
- Love
- Happiness
- Strength
- Good communication
- Determination
- Inner glow
- Focus
- Openness to advice
- Creativity
- Passion
- Enthusiasm
- Command
- Energy
- Fun
- Leadership
- Love

Which of these qualities do you have? Write them down. (Note that some are listed more than once because they are so crucial to your ZEST—more on that in a bit.)

Which qualities do you have in common with these women? We can't always see our own beauty and strength, so ask for help from the people who love you and who you trust. Can you now see the qualities that have given you strength in your life?

You should know the qualities you would like to improve and expand upon. For example, if you want to be more creative, you may want to take an art class, a dance class, or a cooking class. If you want more leadership skills, offer to teach something that you can do well. If you want to refine and enhance your communication skills, don't simply read, but study the next chapter, and then practice and implement what it says.

Which qualities are you developing and expanding to become a powerful woman? Write them down.

Affirmation:
I am a powerful woman.
I embody (name three of your qualities).

YOUR POWER-FILLED STORIES

You are in power when you:

- Feel fulfilled.

- Have clearly defined dreams and desires.

- Feel confident.

- Brim with gratitude.

- Are comfortable with yourself.

- Are doing what you love and loving what you do.

- Are loving every aspect of yourself.

- Say "no" when you need to.

- Say "yes" when you want to.

- Treat yourself and others with kindness.

- Feel satisfied with what you are doing.

- Are pleased that you are doing the right thing for you.

- Are triumphant in overcoming obstacles and challenges with grace.

- Appreciate that problems are the source of power and power-filled stories.

- Are content that you play your own drum and move to the beat of your own music.

We clearly see and admire powerful women, and we enjoy hearing their success stories. Previously, you found the qualities of powerful women. Where did their power come from? It came from *love*. Did you notice that *love* is listed three times? It's that important. As I stated at the beginning of Chapter One, there are *Seven Secrets of Women with ZEST*. Here is the first:

Secret #1 Powerful women love themselves enough to stand strong in their personal power.

*"Love is the purpose, passion, and
source energy that stands firmly within
powerful women. True power comes from love."*

ZEST is the energy, power, and strength that you hold in the world. It is visible when you are faced with an enormous challenge. You don't know how you are going to manage the situation or survive, but you do. You pull all your true power together to do what needs to be done.

Have you ever done something that you did not think you were strong enough and/or capable enough to do? Did you look back later at that event, and were you astonished by your accomplishment? That's a time of power; that's one of your power-filled stories. Tap into these experiences to remind yourself of your strength and capability. These stories give you courage—and remind and validate that you are a woman of power and strength.

ACCESSING YOUR POWER-FILLED STORIES

Next is a two-part exercise to harvest your power-filled stories. This can be done alone, but it's so much more fun to share with other people.

Keep in mind that power-filled moments are unique for each of us—and personal. What others think of your power-filled stories does not matter. If you are working with a group, allow others the courtesy of supporting their stories.

- Part 1: Look back on your life and identify moments or times when you felt most powerful—when you felt like a powerful woman. Think of a time that reflects whatever you define as power. It might be a goal that you set and accomplished or an unexpected tragedy that you overcame. What power-filled stories come to your mind? Stay in each story until you can feel it in your body. Journal each story and include your feelings.

- Part 2: Go back in time and see if you can find the first power-filled story of your life. Write it down, and include your feelings. Your first power-filled story reinforces your understanding and anchors your belief that you have been powerful for a very long time. It was inside of you even when you were not aware of it. Being a woman of power is in your DNA. Your matriarchal ancestors had these special qualities; if they did not they wouldn't have survived and you wouldn't be here now.

Are there similarities in your power-filled stories? Courage, leadership, speaking your mind, or standing up for what you believe in? What personal qualities were prominent? Go back to the list in this chapter as needed, or create your own list.

By discovering your power-filled stories, you find the person you were born to be. This is important because it is your powerful woman who has the courage to dream. It is your powerful woman who makes your dreams come true. When you are in your power, you wear no masks; you are your authentic self. Hold that feeling, and you expand your power. Feel it in your womb and in your heart.

The other night, my power stories came back to me in a dream. It was a replay of all the nice things anyone and everyone has ever said or written to me in my entire life. I saw myself as a child being complimented for my penmanship, at a job interview when I was told that I was the answer to the employer's dreams, and when I felt the touch of a child's hand on my face as the child said, "I love you." I don't know what triggered that dream, but I spent the next few days feeling the warm glow. I'm feeling it now as I replay these moments in my life.

Thinking and talking about your power-filled stories creates a gain in energy. In his book *Biology of Belief*, Bruce Lipton explains that how you think of yourself and how you speak about yourself has an impact on your body at the molecular level. He asks: "What would your life be like if you learned that you are more powerful than you have ever been taught?"

Start practicing replaying the power-filled memories. Research shows that recalling positive experiences increases endorphins, so this is right on track with science. It's a sure way to eliminate the habitual replaying of stories of your saddest, most difficult moments. We'll talk more about this again in Chapter Six, *Barriers to Emotional* ZEST. You feel good when you think of your power stories. Take a moment and congratulate yourself that you have power stories.

Affirmation:

I feel my love, courage, and strength in my power-filled stories.

RELATIONSHIPS

*"The purpose of relationship is not to have another
who might complete you, but to have another with
whom you might share your completeness."*
—*Neale Donald Walsch*

Relationships are everywhere and they are everything. They are necessary for growth, evolution, and development. The meaning of life can be found in personal relationships. They are why humans are here on this planet at this time. By definition, relationship is the state of being connected. I personally believe that relationships may start as early as the moment of conception—and continue well after we are no longer living. Even death cannot separate relationships.

Men and women both have roles in the creation of a balanced world. A well-documented and widely discussed quantum evolutionary shift began a few years before 2012 and has been continuing for many years. It is a time of deep transformation for the self and others to unite feminine and masculine energies. It is a time for women and men to embrace feminine renewal, appreciation, and harmonizing of the universal energies—without sacrificing the male energy. Now is the time to balance the energies—not to flip them into the female equivalent of dominance, but into a co-created, balanced culture.

The balance of energies can be seen in a new, evolving parenting model that is not likely how the parents themselves were raised. In many modern, two parent homes, the care and nurturing of the children is a shared responsibility. However, these parents were on their own to figure out how to coparent in a more nurturing way.

Ironically, divorce is forcing men and women into coparenting roles; they become both the mother and the father to their children. Balanced parenting should not have to happen only in divorced families. In order for this to happen on a global scale, men and women must relearn to honor and respect each other and hold themselves in a new, radiant light.

"Live so that when your children think of fairness,
caring, and integrity, they think of you."
—H. Jackson Brown Jr.

The relationship between parents may be reflected in their children. Would you rather live in a household with domineering or emotionally absent members or in a cooperative, caring, and loving household?

Power in relationships isn't always balanced. A partner who makes all of the decisions and seeks control is not contributing positively to a relationship. Being controlled and having no personal freedom is exhausting. Controlling someone else and making all the decisions also takes a great deal of energy. Let me put it this way: if you're standing with your foot on someone's neck (figuratively speaking), neither one of you can move. You may be controlling that person and preventing his or her movement and behavior, but you are not free either.

Manipulation is not power. A mother who teaches her children how to manipulate their father to get what they want or what she wants is not being wise. Manipulation is an energy loss; it makes you tired and is not sustainable.

Being good at relationships isn't just a nice idea—a "good if you have that" item. It goes beyond important and vital; for me, it is the meaning of life. Power balance in relationships is an energy gain that makes you feel satisfied, happy, and abundant.

Many years ago, I wasn't very good at relationships. My challenge was that my personal power was too big, unwieldy, and out of balance. I didn't know how to align my emotional, physical, and mental resources. I had difficulty getting along with people. If they were strong and confident it usually was fine, but if they were "wimpy" I had no patience for their whining and complaining.

My impact was of the Chef Gordon Ramsay kind. You know who he is? I remember when I was in my twenties going to a party, and taking it upon myself to rearrange the chairs on the deck. Not everyone could sit comfortably the way the deck chairs were set up. I thought I was doing a good thing. "Move this chair here, move that one there. Isn't that better?" Now, we could make maximum use of the space, and everyone could have a comfortable seat.

The silent response to my behavior was clear when I was the only one left sitting on the deck, and everyone else had gone inside. I was so embarrassed. In the moment, I was clueless that I was perceived by some people as really negative or bossy.

At that time, I had a wonderful boss and mentor who could see my potential, but I still had a lot of sharp edges. She called me "a diamond in the rough." She knew that the greatest challenges in my life were around managing my personal power in my relationships.

I often heard: "Shh." "You're too loud." "You're too much." I competed for my place in the pecking order and for control. I got good at it, and it became a habit. It usually wasn't what I said, but the ferocious tone I used. Then I would over analyze every word I had said *after* it was out of my mouth and be racked with guilt. It's not surprising that I was often depressed. It is said that depression is anger turned inward. I didn't like myself, I wasn't happy with myself, and I didn't feel proud of myself.

When I look back, I can only imagine how terrible I made people feel—even though I learned to apologize sincerely and quickly. Most of the time though, that didn't repair the damage to the relationship. If I drop your plate and break it, saying *I'm sorry* isn't going to fix it.

Others noticed my controlling ways too. When I worked at the Department of Justice putting together a conference, one of my colleagues was designing the name tag format. He put them on each person's office door with a little byline. Mine was: Linda Babulic, Tolerates No Fools. That certainly gave people a pause at my door. They weren't all fools, and I still had to work with them.

My title wasn't all bad, of course. I also had support and compliments for my "you tell it like it is; take no crap" attitude. It did serve me well on a few occasions, but my "attitude" was often misdirected and inappropriate.

Another mentor told me: "Linda, you're going to have impact." I was thrilled, but only for a moment. Then, she finished, "You need to decide what that impact will be, and what it will look like." She had seen me in action.

I'm pleased that things have gotten better. I got to know my personal power intimately, how it feels, what makes it big, and what makes it small. I studied the impact of others. I saw that doing a little thing can make a big difference in someone's life. Remember the woman on the bus?

Once I understood how to manage my energy and power, I could be my authentic self; I was accepted more, I was criticized less, and I experienced much healthier relationships.

You have many relationships that you can explore: relationships to yourself, your emotions, your body, your mind, your spirituality, and your sexual self. You have relationships with the people in your family, your life, and your work.

Decide who *you* want to be in your relationships—and how *you* want to feel.

Can you speak your truth in *all* of your relationships? How about *some* or *any*? Perhaps you can speak the truth in some relationships—while not in others or not to the same level. Do you get together with a certain friend because saying "no" would create a conflict? Do you have some friends to whom you can say that you would rather stay home at night? They're okay with that, and they understand? How does your vision of being a powerful woman coexist in your relationships?

I once knew a woman who was having an affair with a man who was engaged to another woman. For some, this may be astounding; they may try to apply their personal beliefs and values to understand why he would maintain his engagement with one women while having an affair with another. Of course, I asked the woman why she was in the relationship. The woman's response was this, "He's a wonderful man and a great lover; he's just not very good at relationships!"

Relationships are closest to you when they have the greatest effect on you and how you live your life. The people in your life give you energy and/or you give them energy because you have varying attachments to each other. Earlier you relived your power-filled stories. Do you hold positive or negative memories of the reaction others had to your power and success? What was the reaction when your powerful ZEST was fully expressed and your power-filled story was actualized?

Lake Meditation—Relationships

To discover the emotional impact and influence connected to your immediate relationships, the following Lake Meditation exercise may help. Go to www.ZESTyourLife.com/extras for a free recording of this meditation.

The Lake Meditation—15 Minutes

Play some soft music—something that does not hold an emotional charge for you. Get comfortable. Know that you are safe, powerful, and courageous. You are completely grounded, strong, and calm.

Imagine that you are at your favorite lake. The water is calm, the sun is shining, and there is no one around. You walk into the water a little way. As you gaze into the water, you see an image of yourself.

- What do you see when you look at yourself?
- What feelings do you have?
- What stories do you tell about yourself?
- Are you wearing a mask, or do you see your authentic self?

Your image now disappears.

Come back to shore for a moment, and capture your impressions by journaling them.

You walk back into the water a little way. As you gaze into the water, you see an image of your father.

- Can you be yourself when you are with your father?
- What does he expect of you?
- What feelings do you have?
- What masks do you wear when you are with him?

The image of your father now disappears.

Come back to shore for a moment, and capture your impressions by writing them down.

Again walk back in the water. As you gaze into the water, you now see an image of your mother.

- Can you be yourself when you are with your mother?
- What does she expect of you?
- What feelings do you have?

- What masks do you wear when you are with her?

The image of your mother now disappears.

You're back on the shore. Capture your impressions by making a note of them.

Walk in the water a little way. As you gaze into the water, you see an image of your siblings and/or significant other. Be with them one at a time—each brother, sister, and significant other—anyone who has had significant impact on what you think of yourself. The significant other could be a step-parent, aunt, partner, co-worker, and/or boss.

- Can you be yourself when you are with them?

- What do they expect of you?

- What feelings do you have?

- What masks do you wear when you are with them?

The image now disappears.

Come back to shore for a moment, and capture your impressions by writing them down.

And one last time you walk into the water a little way. As you gaze into the water, you see yourself again.

- What feelings do you have?

Say, "Thank you. I love you."

Your image now disappears.

Come back to shore for a moment, and capture your impressions by journaling them.

At the lake, dip your hands in the water, and wash your face and arms. Take a deep breath, walk out of the water, and return. Take another nice, deep breath.

While doing the Lake Meditation exercise, did you see some positive, uplifting images? You may have discovered that you are a strong, powerful woman. Did you open your heart to your father, mother, sibling, and significant other? You stood in your beauty and your majesty, and that feels great.

Some of the images you saw at the lake may no longer hold any emotional charge for you. Just by looking at them, the emotions attached to them have dissolved like the images in the water.

Most often, the Lake Meditation exercise manifests a mixture of both positive and negative images and feelings. It can provide a mirror for who we are and how we perceive ourselves. Revisiting our relationships can make sense out of the past and break limiting beliefs that we may have formed about ourselves and others. It can be the first step in dismantling the barriers that have been holding us back from our authentic selves. The purpose is healing, not traumatizing. What are you feeling now and why? Take a moment to hold yourself in love, compassion, and joy.

Affirmation:
I breathe in life, I breathe in love.
Love is all around me.

Using positive power in a relationship can be extremely rewarding for everyone. It puts the relationship in energetic balance.

Can you see positive power within yourself? If you cannot see it within yourself, you are not emitting it to others, and you cannot see it in others. Review your power-filled woman qualities to remind yourself of what you can do and see them within yourself.

What can you do to be in your power in your relationships? Now is the time to look at each and every one of them and make sure that you create or recreate the kind of relationships you want in your life. If you want love, joy, and support in your relationships, then you must bring them to your relationships. Be the kind of person you want to come home to, and you'll attract the relationships that you desire. Set your intent to attract relationships that contribute to creating the life you want.

Relationships help you discover who you are. You have the right to choose the kind of life that you want for yourself. You are blessed with relationships and must honor this privilege by living your life fully, consciously, and responsibly. The power and impact of your actions on yourself, your life, and others is far greater than you may imagine. Can you love and awaken the woman within—the one you never show to the world—enough to bring her out?

"The easiest kind of relationship for me is with ten thousand people. The hardest is with one."
—*Joan Baez*

THE PEOPLE YOU SPEND THE MOST TIME WITH

Have you noticed that, as you have grown and evolved, you have developed new relationships more in keeping with the mindset and lifestyle that you have now? Do you and the people you are with experience a gain of energy when you are together? If your friends are making you tired and bringing you down, you may want to consider making some changes.

Motivational speaker Jim Rohn said, "You become the average of the five people you spend the most time with. You will have the average of their income, health, lifestyle, and relationships." (Quote by Jim Rohn, America's Foremost Business Philosopher, reprinted with permission from Jim Rohn International. As a world-renowned author and success expert, Jim Rohn touched millions of lives during his forty-six year career as a motivational speaker and messenger of positive life change. For more information on Jim and his popular personal achievement resources or to subscribe to the weekly Jim Rohn Newsletter, visit www.JimRohn.com.)

Who are the five people with whom you spend the most time?

1.

2.

3.

4.

5.

List the qualities and values that you would like to emulate. Find people with these qualities, and spend time with them. You can also find people who are doing better in the areas you want to improve in, and spend time with them.

I don't know where it came from, but I remember the saying: "I'll be back. When I'm with you, I feel better about myself." When you are with someone, can he or she say that to you? Can you say it in return?

"Too often we underestimate the power of a touch, a smile, a kind word, a listening ear, an honest compliment, or the smallest act of caring, all of which have the potential to turn a life around."

—*Leo Buscaglia*

COUNCIL OF WISE WOMEN

Create a council of wise women by making a list of eight women who have eight qualities you would like to have or expand upon. You don't need to know these women personally; they can be women from anywhere and anytime. You may want to gather photos of them and create a visual circle of your council. Close your eyes, and meet with them one on one in your mind and heart to ask if they would help you develop the qualities they possess. See each woman in front of you; she is smiling and appreciates that you thought to ask her. They each said yes, because they love and support you. Open your heart with gratitude. You can relax; there is no need to be defensive.

Gather these women together, and mentally convene a wise woman council meeting. Imagine how they look, what they are wearing, what you are wearing, if you are outside or inside, and how everything looks. If you are inside, is there a fireplace? Are you sitting on the floor or in chairs? Open the meeting by thanking them all for agreeing to help you. For example, if you would like more grace in your life, the wise woman who brings that gift says a few words, then the woman on her right adds her wisdom, and so on around the circle. Listen and receive the advice and guidance they are gifting you. Let it affect you, even change you as it comes into you. Notice what comes to light and even seems like your very own thoughts.

Thank them and end the meeting by opening the circle: "The circle is opened, but unbroken."

Take the knowledge that you now have about grace, and pay attention to how it shows up for you in the next week. It may be in movies, magazines, or conversations. Allow some time for the quality of grace to be integrated into you. Convene the wise woman circle for each quality you are developing or expanding.

This is now part of the womb wisdom that you carry and can share with others. My mother-in-law used to say, "We each carry our own bundle." Womb wisdom is the healing bundle you carry for yourself and others. It cultivates, nurtures, and supports your positive relationships.

You can also create a physical council of wise people to provide advice to you on any major decision you are faced with. My client was seriously considering buying the first franchise of a women's magazine. She was very conflicted because she was working with and was a friend of the magazine's founder. On very short notice, a group of women from very diverse backgrounds gathered in a private room in a restaurant. My client was very touched that so many people cared about her and her welfare. She presented why she wanted to buy the franchise, the financial costs, and the potential revenue. Each of us gave her the knowledge that we had about what this would do to her life, what she had to gain, and what she had to lose. In the end, it was unanimous: owning a magazine is not glamorous—it's about selling advertising. She digested and used the advice, and is very happy with her decision to not buy the franchise.

Affirmation:
My life and my relationships are enriching,
stimulating, and fun!

Through your power stories, you know and feel your inner power, the strength of your womb, and your qualities. You have a plan to develop the qualities you want to establish and expand. Knowing your power intimately gives you the ability to focus your dreams and desires so that you can live your ideal life.

It takes courage to challenge fears, beliefs, and barriers, to admit that they are holding you back, and to be willing to make the necessary changes. Your council of wise women is ready to help and guide you. Keep them close at hand as you seek authenticity in the next chapter.

Chapter 2
Finding Authenticity

"The sun is shining; it's time to remove the clouds."

ZEST is generated by being your authentic self—the person you were meant to be. When you were a child, you were your authentic self. To safely bring your shining self out of hiding and into the light, you first need to find the barriers and beliefs that diminished or shut down your true, real, and actual self. That person may be covered up, but she still exists.

Somewhere in your developmental years, you had ZEST; then you were told to stuff it away. You may have been told to be quiet, stop talking, or speak up and not be so shy. As an adult, are you told that you are "too much", that you can be intimidating, or that you're not "social" enough?

Now you know that pushing your authentic self away is not a good idea because it depletes your energy in your emotional, physical, mental, and spiritual aspects. Have you noticed that you're tired, lack focus, and often get sick when you can't be yourself and do what is best for you? I used to get terrible migraine headaches or stomach aches.

Let's explore the various aspects of your makeup and how you are being affected:

- Emotionally. Do you rely on others to make you happy? Do you need their approval? Can you go a day without spending money?

- Physically. Are you out of breath when walking a distance? Do you have trouble spending a day without a cigarette, coffee, alcohol, or sugar?

- Mentally. Are you sad, depressed, or miserable? Have you asked for help from a professional?

- Spiritually. Are you disconnected from your authentic self, your higher self?

WHO HAS YOUR POWER?

Blaming others for the problems in your life puts you in a powerless place. It gives your problems power and control over your life. No one has power and autonomy if she does not take her life, dreams, and desires as her own responsibility. When you give someone else the responsibility for your life, your dreams, and your happiness, you also give away your power to have what you really want.

If you don't have the life you want, who have you given that responsibility to? Who has your power? Have you given your power to others? You don't mean to do it, but it happens and it can become a barrier to ZEST.

For example, Karen, an office supervisor, was sick and away from the office for a year. Before she left, she divided her duties between Mary and Carol, the two women who reported to her. Karen confided in me that the office dynamic she came back to was entirely different from the one she had left. Mary resented that Karen, her supervisor, had returned to assume her responsibilities. Karen would review the duties with the staff, but the next morning she would be told by Steven, her boss, that Mary didn't need to do those things. Karen was feeling powerless and frustrated.

It didn't take Karen long to figure out what was going on. She noticed that Mary was staying late after work. It turned out that she had gained Steven's favor because they were having an affair. As soon as I pointed out to Karen that she no longer held her own power, she changed her attitude and took it back. She was clear and focused on the situation she had to address. With Steven's consent, she communicated clearly what the lines of reporting were. Everyone agreed, and the office ran smoothly again.

The influences and forces that stop you only do so because you let them. Your life is your responsibility—not the responsibility of other people or luck. Take your power back and vow never to hand it over to anyone else. The circumstances of your life, as well as what and who is in your life are your own creations.

Take responsibility for your life and dreams. Choose the ability to respond and you have the power to change your life. To change your life, you must take responsibility for it. Look at every situation from the perspective of the strong, mature, and wise woman that you are now.

When you change your perception of the past, you change your life in the present moment. You can change your perception of the past, even if it was something negative that caused you to let go of your power.

A client of mine recently did this. When she was young, her mother had tried to kill her. Sitting at the kitchen table with her siblings, her mother picked up a knife and threw it at her. Afterward, she hid her bleeding hand from her mother and she fell silent. In her six-year-old state of mind, she concluded that her mother had just tried to kill her.

For her fifty-first birthday, this client decided to give herself a gift. She wanted to let go of this story because every time she thought about it and told it, it drained her energy. She kept replaying the painful memories over and over again. She knew that this incident had changed her and restricted her joy and specifically her laughter. It was time for her to change her beliefs about the event so that she could reframe and understand it from an adult perspective. Here are some of the questions that I asked her and her new perceptions:

- Were you sitting quietly at the table? *No, I was probably laughing and fooling around with my brothers and sisters.*

- She was an exuberant child filled with lively energy, and her mother was probably out of patience with her noise and wanted her to stop.

- If you were cut and bleeding seriously and unable to hide it, what would your mother have done? *She would have bandaged me up.*

- Your mother is smart woman. If she wanted to kill you, would she have chosen to do it by throwing a knife at you in the kitchen?

She had to chuckle at how little sense this made. Her mother was not trying to kill her.

This story is kind of disturbing since most mothers do not throw knives at their children because they are out of patience or want them to be quiet. Believing that her mother tried to kill her made her fear her mother and live as a victim and a helpless child. As an adult it meant that she had lost her personal power and given it to her mother. She felt angry and believed that her mother controlled and manipulated her. Having the courage to evaluate and change her beliefs, and let go of the fear that was attached to the old story brought her the comfort, confidence, and joy she had been seeking for a long time.

Cleaning up our mental messes creates a gain in power and energy. When you change your perception of the past, you change your life in the present moment.

Cleaning up the mess is the short-term remedy, but not the solution. Sometimes, we need the help of therapy and/or medication to get us to the long-term solution of living a new life with emotional ZEST!

When you are not a powerful woman with ZEST, it is costing you your youth, vitality, and your authentic self. Not being in your ZEST is making you age at a rapid rate and zapping your energy. If you don't believe that you are worthy and deserving of becoming a powerful woman, you're wrong.

It's time to say: "Stop, enough!" End the pattern of fear and giving away your power. Remove fears that are barring you and blocking you from your joy, vibrancy, and happiness. As I stated at the beginning of Chapter One, there are *Seven Secrets of Women with ZEST*. Here is the second secret: **Secret #2 Powerful women don't let fear stop them.**

Others have done it and you can too.

Reclaim your power, and make use of it in your life to make your family, your community, and the world a better place. You are worthy and deserve to be a powerful woman. Now is the time to make your life functional.

Affirmation:
I honor and respect myself as a brave,
courageous, and powerful woman with ZEST.

Your Ideal Life

Start right now to imagine your ideal life.

- If you could magically have everything you wanted, what would your ideal life look like?

- What are you doing in your ideal life?

- What have you dreamed of doing?

- Where are you living—in the city, in the country, or do you have a home in both?

- What country are you living in?

- Who are the people in your ideal life?

- Who are the five people that you spend the most time with?

- How do they support your wholeness?

Your ideals have a big impact on your income, health, lifestyle, and relationships. Choose them wisely.

Imagine the feelings of satisfaction, fulfillment, and happiness in your ideal life now that you have created a supportive structure for your ideas and ideals.

CHAPTER 3
COMMUNICATION

"Intuition occurs when we directly perceive facts outside the range of the usual five senses and independently of any reasoning process."
—Mona Lisa Schulz, MD, PhD

Intuition is the highest level of human communication. It is the inner knowing and dialogue that you receive to help you make decisions that are not based on linear thinking or logic. Intuitive knowledge comes from dreams, feelings, body twitches, or gut feelings. You must listen to all of these things.

While I was in Bolivia and hiking to Machu Picchu in Peru, I had a "feeling" that something had happened to my mother-in-law. I was able to email home from the hotel in Cuzco to ask how she was. However, my family had decided that the bad news could wait, so they didn't tell me what had happened. After being across the world, on my own for three weeks, the first question I asked my husband on the ride home from the airport was, "What happened to your mother?" I knew something had happened; I thought she might have even passed away; she was in her nineties. However, I was relieved to hear she was recovering; she had fallen and broken her hip.

Intuition is a major component of how I communicate. I rely on and trust my intuition to guide me and help me know when to say something, what to say, and how to say it. Entire sections of this book have been written intuitively by listening and following my heart. Intuition is communication with your higher self.

I included this chapter about communication because good communication is a tool, a vehicle, and a necessary quality to having ZEST in your life. Do you remember one of the qualities of a powerful woman? She's a good communicator. If she wasn't, how would we know her qualities? We all must become proficient in heart-to-heart communication in order to learn to love ourselves, others, and the world around us.

If I can't communicate with myself openly and honestly, then what am I doing here, and how am I ever going to communicate with anyone else? I want to communicate to make a difference and have impact. I can only do that when I do it well.

So many of us are connected electronically by Internet, email, or Facebook—and sometimes that gives us a global connection that generations before us could never have. It's all communication, and the best communication is from the heart; that's where your ZEST comes from. Communication connects our humanity.

> *"Reading and writing are both forms of communication.*
> *So are speaking and listening.*
> *In fact, those are the four basic types of communication.*
> *And think of all the hours you spend doing at least one of those four things, the ability to do them well is absolutely critical to your effectiveness."*
> —*Dr. Stephen R. Covey*

Communication's main components are listening, understanding, and responding. A great number of problems in relationships are caused by miscommunication and misunderstanding.

Relationships are greatly enhanced with effective communication. Effective communication focuses on creating understanding by listening effectively and using judicious questioning techniques. Knowing the impact of verbal communication and non-verbal communication ensures that you say what you mean and mean what you say.

"Without communication there is no relationship."
—Nadine Lalonde, ZEST Your Life program participant

ACTIVE LISTENING

We spend most of our waking hours communicating. We learn how to speak, read, and write—but have you learned how to listen?

"Listening involves hearing the speaker's words, understanding the message and its importance to the speaker, and communicating that understanding to the speaker...

It is key to developing and maintaining relationships, making decisions, and solving problems. Listening is such a part of our everyday lives, both at work and at home, that sometimes we take it for granted."
—Successful Manager's Handbook

Think back on conversations when you felt like someone was really listening to you. Close your eyes, relax, and notice how were you feeling.

- What was the other person(s) doing? Paraphrasing, questioning, encouraging you to continue talking?

- Did the other person make you feel worthwhile, important, comfortable, understood, and recognized?

Good listeners pay attention to what is said and how it is said. They watch for the non-verbal messages and read "between the lines" to seek support for or contradictions to the verbal messages. They focus on the similarities and connections to find common ground and use the differences to understand the situations.

> *"If you think communication is all talk, you haven't been listening."*
>
> —*Ashleigh Brilliant, www.AshleighBrilliant.com*

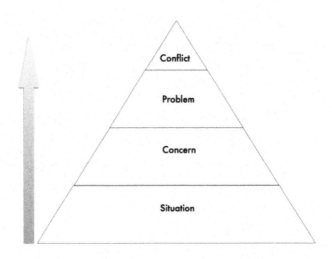

Situation escalation illustration by Linda Babulic

Every day we encounter and resolve dozens of situations. When a situation is not resolved it can become a concern, then a problem, and can escalate into a conflict. The source of the issue is not when and where it shows up; it is always before. The source of the conflict exists before the conflict itself appears.

Here's a simple example. A couple of children are playing nicely all afternoon. Around three o'clock, they start to raise their voices at each other. Then it escalates to yelling, crying, and complaining. The problem appears to be that the children are not getting along. Give them a healthy snack, and they go back to playing nicely. The source of the conflict - they were hungry - existed before they started to raise their voices. By the way, this works with adults too! Feed them and yourself before there is a conflict.

Have you ever been in the awkward position where someone you were with became totally frustrated and angry? Active listening is a good strategy to help you manage this uncomfortable dilemma.

Although most people won't be threatening or physically aggressive, trust your instincts to protect yourself. If you feel like you're in danger then leave the area immediately without hesitation and without saying anything else to that person.

Whether the person is angry or not, take a deep breath, calm yourself, and listen. Listen with an open heart so that you understand what the other person is trying to tell you. Let that person repeat himself or herself and "get it all out". Don't interrupt, and don't rehearse a rebuttal in your head. Listen past the words; listen to the feelings and the meaning, as well as the content. What is this person really trying to tell you? "Does your dog bite?" can mean "I am afraid." *Plan first to understand, then to be understood.*

Notice your listening viewpoint: sitting, standing, beside, in front, or behind. When possible, put yourself on the same physical level as the person you are conversing with.

Studies have shown that generally women like to be face to face and men are more comfortable side by side during a conversation. When I was teaching my corporate training program, one of my students put this to the test. A male supervisor came to class with a story about what happened when he was speaking with a female coworker. They were standing in front of a piece of machinery that they were discussing. He tried several times to stand beside her, but she kept putting herself in front of him. He was astute enough to notice that she became agitated when they were side by side and was calmer when they were face-to-face.

Mona Lisa Schulz, MD, PhD, neuropsychiatrist, neuroscientist, medical intuitive, and author of *Awakening Intuition,* summarized an article by Roger A. Drake, Department of Psychology, Western State College of Colorado, Gunnison, Colorado, published in the *International Journal of Neuroscience*:

> One scientist noted something interesting when he was driving with his wife in England. Sitting on the right-hand side at the steering wheel, with his wife in the passenger seat on his left, he found that he was far more receptive to his wife's conversation, including her directions and instruction on his driving, than he was at home in the United States, where she sat on his right. In England, she was talking into his left ear and to his *right* brain and was much more easily able to persuade him of her points. In England, he did whatever she wanted. Back home, however, he was back in the driver's seat in every sense. In America, where his wife spoke into his right ear to his *left* brain, he was far more resistant to her suggestions. His left brain could assert control over the situation. He didn't listen to his wife anymore. No wonder men always want to do the driving in the United States!

Put yourself in the other person's place; how do you want to be treated? It's perfectly appropriate to say: "I'm sorry you're upset." Although the situation may not be your fault, saying you're sorry can often can calm a person down. Telling someone to "calm down" can be like pouring gasoline on a fire.

To improve your relationship, keep the conversation in control; don't back off, be totally responsible, look the person in the eyes, and connect. Say to the other person: "I care about you; tell me what I can do to help this situation," or "Is there anything I can do?" For many, offering moral support helps the person recognize that someone cares about how he or she feels.

Don't assume that you know what others are thinking or what they mean when they say something or look a certain way. One of the most difficult things we have to do as humans is to hold onto our own emotions when someone else is not. Old patterns, beliefs, and behaviors jump in and can cause irreparable damage. Stop blaming the other person. Don't be the teacher who blames the student for not learning.

It is important to remember that the key to effective listening is to not turn off your speakers. Acknowledge what they say. Give them thanks and praise, "Thanks for having this conversation with me. I feel better now that I am starting to understand how you feel." Remember when you felt really listened to, and try to emulate what you received.

Don't forget to breathe!

Affirmation:

**I pay attention to what
is said and to how it is said.**

UNDERSTANDING

*"To understand, we must uncover emotion and factual content.
Words alone can be misleading…Communication is a process where messages
are sent and received from one person to another. Messages contain two
parts—factual content and personal emotion. Words can be heard and
actions seen, but we can only infer what these words and actions mean. Most
of us keep our emotions and thoughts private and hidden; however, clues to
feelings can be found in behaviors if we probe to uncover them."*
—Cheryl A. Picard

THE INCONSISTENT MESSAGE

To build relationships, we need to know how effective and believable we are when we communicate face-to-face. Professor Mehrabian, Ph.D. (retired), while at UCLA, looked at the connections between the only three elements that are communicated each time we speak: the verbal, vocal, and visual elements. He measured the difference between what part of our message is most believed when we speak to someone face-to-face about feelings and attitudes, such as like and dislike.

When you are speaking to another person, that person is experiencing these three elements and deciding whether you are believable and likable:

- The *verbal* element is the message itself: *the words that you say.*

- The *vocal* element is the tone of your voice: *high, low, nasal, squeaky or all the same tone.*

- The *visual* element is what people see: *your facial expressions and body language.*

The research found that if these three elements are all saying the same thing, then the person communicating is more believable than if the message being portrayed from these elements is inconsistent. If you're saying yes while shaking your head no, that affects your believability.

Write your estimate of which of these elements carries the most believability when you are speaking face-to-face (interpersonal communication) to persuade a listener:

_____%—Words that you say: verbal

_____%— Element in your voice: vocal

_____%— What they see: visual and facial

Total   100%

Professor Mehrabian's research, contained in his book, *Silent Messages,* was based on what individuals believed while witnessing an inconsistent message. If the message was consistent, all three elements would work together. The excitement and enthusiasm of the voice combined with the energy and animation of the face and body to reflect the confidence and conviction of what was said. The words, the voice, and the delivery were all in alignment, and the message got through.

When we are nervous, awkward, or under pressure we tend to block our content and give an inconsistent message. For example, someone who looks downward, speaks in a halting and tremulous voice, and clasps his or her hands in front of them is giving a specific message. If that person then says, "I am excited to be here," the words are not be believed due to the inconsistency.

Here's what they found people believe:

7 %—Words that you say: verbal

38%— Element in your voice: vocal

55%— What they see: visual and facial

TOTAL   100%

Adapted from *The Art of Communicating,* by Bert Decker, Crisp Publications.

Greet people warmly with a smile and an open heart. Positive, consistent communication is a skill and quality of every powerful ZESTY woman. With practice and focus, you can master it. Summarizing what the person has said and stating your understanding is a useful technique. Information is more easily remembered by associating what is said with something familiar to you and repeating the information internally or out loud. If additional clarity is required, ask questions.

Your effectiveness depends largely on how well you can understand the needs and desires of the person you are communicating with—as well as how clearly you can make your own needs known and how easily and fully others can comprehend what you are communicating. To do this, you must first be able to organize your own thinking in a logical and easily communicated structure.

It's up to you to help the people around you do the same thing. Asking the right questions helps others understand and clarify their thinking about the subject. *Clarity of thinking and clarity of communication are two sides of the same golden coin.*

Sometimes the phrases we use can be a bad habit and are hard to break. Speaking sarcastically is a habit. Let's see if these questions are familiar to you:

- Why in the world would you do that?

- Don't you know that won't work?

- Is that really what you think?

- How can you even think that?

- Who told you that?

- Can you prove that?

Can you surmise why asking sarcastic questions is not likely to move the conversation ahead in a positive direction?

QUESTIONS

Asking good questions is a powerful tool. Questions that focus and clarify lead to understanding.

There are several different kinds of questions, and they each serve a different purpose and produce a different result.

- Closed-ended Questions. Closed-ended questions can be answered with a yes or no or by making a single selection. Example: "Do you want the red one or the green one?" If you want a more comprehensive answer, then choose another style of question.

- Open-ended Questions. Open-ended questions have no "correct answer." They allow the individuals to talk more and generate discussion. When using open-ended questions be prepared to listen and take whatever time is needed to complete the conversation to everyone's satisfaction. Start questions with:

  - What
  - Which
  - How much
  - How many
  - Who
  - When
  - Where
  - Why
  - If

The danger with open-ended questions is that the person may ramble and go off on a tangent, forgetting the question you asked. When this happens, gently remind that person of the question by using probing questions.

- Probing Questions. Probing questions are more specific than open-ended questions, but still open. Use them to funnel the direction of the discussion. For example: "Where do you think improvements could be made to...?" This works effectively to get someone to stop complaining about a problem and focus on possible solutions.

- Specific Questions. When certain information is sought, use specific questions. For example: "What happened when Mary asked Jane to...?" Be prepared to have a different point of view when you ask the same question to someone else. Turn your active listening skills to the maximum and discern what feelings are involved and where any miscommunication may have occurred.

- Leading Questions. Leading questions invite the answer that is expected. For example: "Do you not agree that we should not drink and drive?" Some people use leading questions in heated discussions or arguments. Personally, I don't like when this is done; it makes me feel like I'm being tricked into agreeing to something.

Softeners to Begin Questions

Just out of curiosity...

By the way...

Just offhand...

In your view...

In your opinion...

Normally...

Approximately...

TIP: Use the person's first name when you are speaking. It personalizes the conversation. Use it sparingly; you don't want to sound like you're delivering a sales pitch.

- Judicious Questions. These are my favorite. Judicious equals discreet, skillful, and discerning. These are questions that focus, clarify, and bridge. They allow you to probe for understanding, depth, and insight. Keep in mind that some questions don't need an answer; they are questions to live with for a while.

Sample judicious questions:

- Why? Why not?

- What is the best that could happen?

- What is the worst that could happen?

- What do you know for sure?

- How did that make you feel?

- What happened? It sounds like…Is that accurate?

- What does that mean for you?

- How could that work for you?

- If you could have exactly what you want, what would it look like?

- Why can't you have what you want?

- How could you make that happen?

- How can I help make that happen?

- How is that significant?

- Was that good or bad?

- What did you learn from that?

- How do you account for that?

- Why is that?

- What's the pattern here?

- Help me to understand how…what…where…?

- How does that align with your values?

- How can I help you or support you with this?

- What else is there about this?

- Where is this on your priority list?

Ask yourself before you speak, "Whose voice is that in my head?" Sometimes it is our parent's words, opinions, and attitudes that we repeat. Check if this is really what *you* think.

The right kinds of questions help to clarify the understanding of the other person's point of view and feelings, as well as your own. Asking the right questions also guides you to a clear response that benefits everyone.

TIME AND PLACE

We've all made the mistake of trying to have a conversation when the timing was so bad that the whole issue got blown up and became worse than when we started. Avoid having important conversations when you or the other person is rushed, tired, or hungry. Drugs, alcohol, or having a hangover are not conducive to fruitful conversations. The best thing to do is to agree to a place where you won't be interrupted or overheard, and set a specific time to both start and end. Choosing the right timing for conversations, particularly difficult conversations, can be productive and satisfying, even if it does not lead to the desired result.

You know it's time to end the conversation when either you or the other person becomes repetitious and is not adding anything new and valuable to the discussion. You may want to reschedule to a more conducive time after each person has had time to think about it. I had a boss who was good at that. Whenever people started repeating what they had previously said, she would graciously let them know that she understood their concerns, and then she would stand up and end the meeting.

LIES

Unfortunately, human communication often includes lies. It's safe to say that we all know people who lie often, and everyone has lied at one time or another. There are many reasons why people lie:

- They don't trust that you are able to handle the truth.

- They're ashamed of what they did or didn't do and are lying to save face.

- They exaggerate or understate the story depending on what they think you want or need to hear and to justify why they lied.

- They want to spare or hurt your feelings.

Being lied to or lying to someone is a major withdrawal that reduces the amount of trust in the relationship. Interestingly enough, even if the person being lied to never knows it, the lier does, and there's an energy loss that is felt by both parties. In retrospect, it creates that feeling that something *wasn't quite right about the situation or the story.* That burden of guilt or suspicion depletes the energy. There's no ZEST in lies.

Knowing that someone has lied to me, lied about me, or said something nasty about me is always difficult. I've wasted a great deal of energy trying to figure this out. Did you ever find out the truth about something months or years after an incident happened? I'm fascinated by the timing of the truth coming out. It's as if the universe or my intuition gives me the truth when I am best able to handle it. I believe that if you are meant to know, sooner or later, the truth appears. The only conclusion I came to is that I may never know why others do what they do and I have to let those situations go.

INTUITION

Things you know
Things you know you know
Things you know that others don't want you to know
But sooner or later when you need to know, you will

Barriers to Effective Communication

"If the behavior is the communication, what is the message?"

Not only the words, but behaviors, actions, body language, and mannerisms, can encourage or impede effective communication. If a partner's behavior includes betraying you, but that person claims to love you, what is the real message shown in the behavior?

What are we communicating when we roll our eyes? How about when we wink, or when we turn away? Are we criticizing, judging, diagnosing? What are we communicating with a gentle touch? Are we caring, comforting, reassuring, etc.?

Did you know that we talk at a rate of about 200 to 250 words per minute, and we listen at a rate of about 300 to 800 words per minute? What is done with that time lag between the talking and the listening strongly influences how we process and react to what is said. While we are listening to others we could get bored and not give them our full attention. We may check out, because they are not being clear. In those cases, we are not actively listening.

Communication is a process, but what actually happens during the process? We want the messages we send to be received. Whether you are the sender or the receiver, there is sometimes a "communications gap". If we understand the gap, then we can work on narrowing and closing it to create better understanding.

Are there barriers to communication in the environment: a time shortage, too much noise, too many interruptions? What are some barriers to effective listening and to understanding? What is going on in "the gap", besides not listening?

- Judging, evaluating, questioning

- Moralizing

- Lecturing, giving logical or illogical arguments

- Minimizing in a patronizing way

- Giving advice, rushing to solutions

- Directing, ordering

- Approving, disapproving, agreeing

- Interrupting

- Using terminology that isn't understood

- Withdrawing, humoring, diverting

- Talking too fast

Observe people communicating and look for the specific, observable behaviors; what are they communicating? Train yourself to observe and understand people in conversations and how they communicate. How do you think each person feels? Is there a big or small communication gap between them? What barriers are impeding good communication?

Remove the barriers to effective communication; open your heart and communicate from a place of love, honesty, and understanding.

Communicate for ZEST

We can't expect others to act, react, or communicate the way we do. People behave differently because of their own personalities, experiences, and interpretations of situations. Some are calm and methodical, while others are in a rush to get it done. We may perceive things that the person didn't mean. Sometimes, things are said that might be regretted.

Effective communication is vital. Communication is power. Practice and hone your intuition and your communication skills to bring you greater awareness, more success, and fewer frustrations.

Communication's main components are: listening, understanding, and responding. Cultivate your active listening skills, gain understanding by asking questions, and open your heart to be aware and awake in all your communications with yourself and others. Within a few weeks, your intuition, inner guidance, and external communications will all upgrade you to a higher level of ZEST.

Chapter 4
Part 1 ZESTERS

ZESTERS are the things you do and actions you take to activate ZEST in your life. These are personal practices that shift your mindset, nourish you, and renew you. Starting today, test each one and monitor the effect on your energy. Later in the book, you will explore other ZESTERS. Practice and make them habits.

- Read your power-filled stories as often as you need; they are reminders of your ZEST.

- Write down new, power-filled stories as they occur.

- Speak kindly to yourself; doing so changes the molecules in your brain.

- Give yourself praise and recognition for all that you accomplish in a day. That includes taking time for yourself.

- Practice being aware of and in control of your power. How does your body feel? Are you standing or sitting a little straighter?

- Grab the power moments and build on the energy. It may be a good time to do something that you don't believe you're capable of doing.

- If you need to, find a hero and walk in her powerful steps until you can walk in your own. Children learn by watching and imitating others, and so can you.

- Spend time in nature. Take a walk and breathe in the scent of the trees and Mother Earth beneath your feet, smell the flowers, or feel the crunch of the snow beneath your feet.

- Be in this moment—feel, breathe, and celebrate your success.

- Listen past what people say to what they mean and what emotion is attached.

- Listen to yourself and feel what emotions are attached to your thoughts.

- Ask, ask, ask—questions are magic.

- Practice heart-to-heart communication with yourself and others daily.

- Try this when you wake up in the middle of the night, and you can't get back to sleep. Ask: "So, what advice do you have for me?" Then listen to yourself.

- Be grateful that you love yourself enough to be here today.

- Smile.

- Sleep.

CALL TO ACTION

Choose a few ZESTERS that you can implement today. Complete this sentence: "I awaken my ZEST by taking action and doing the following:_____"

1.

2.

3.

Now you have awakened the woman within. Yes, you have done it. The woman inside of you can now glimpse your dreams, your desires, and the life that you are creating. You can have a fulfilling, happy life with great relationships, satisfying work, and thriving dreams that will come true—beyond what you can imagine today.

> *"Live your life in such a way that when your feet*
> *hit the floor in the morning,*
> *Satan shudders and says: 'Oh shit…she's awake.'"*
>
> —*Unknown*

PART 2

CREATE EMOTIONAL MATURITY

"Women are so complicated." How many times have you heard that? Instead, I would rather think of our gender as complex, intricate, and elaborate. We are multi-faceted, like diamonds.

Diamonds are made of carbon that crystallized under conditions of extreme temperature and pressure. Like diamonds, we adjust, adapt, and change under the conditions we are exposed to. Girls are transformed into women physically, mentally, sexually, and emotionally. However, we are often judged and labeled as simply "emotional".

Life is emotional and life changes. Would you want it any other way?

"Most of us have no idea how to navigate our brilliant, beautiful, important, and dazzlingly perfect emotions. We feel something deeply and...poof!...we think something is desperately wrong with us. Our balance is gone. We are lost to the abyss.

In fact, for most women, our highest goal for ourselves is a plain, vanilla emotional life. But there is nothing plain and nothing vanilla about a woman."

—Mama Gena www.MamaGenas.com

CHAPTER 5
EMOTIONS

WHAT ARE EMOTIONS?

The word emotion is often defined as a feeling or state of mind. Jung distinguished between feeling (a function which evaluates) and emotion (a physiological affect). Emotions are like the water in the river: flowing, overflowing, stuck in a damn, clear, murky, fluid, frozen, rushing, calm, always in action, and ever-changing.

Let's explore that analogy a little more. When emotions are murky, stuck, or angry, they are like ice—a rigid and solid block of energy—which can't move. Over the years, we develop emotional patterns that are triggered by particular situations and prompt a habitual reaction. On the other hand, we can all relate to when our feelings are clear and granting us a calm, gentle flow.

Trust and understand your emotions and feelings to guide you, but not to control you. Emotions are energy coming to and going from the body—energy in motion. Listen to the information that your feelings provide, and you will be rewarded with a gain in ZEST and energy. Feelings help you understand and respond to the world around you with emotional maturity.

Creating and achieving conscious emotional maturity is the journey from hopeless confused victim, who blames others, can't make decisions, and can't cope with her feelings to the authentic woman who trusts her inner knowing, continuously improves emotional understanding and control, and is able to see what matters and what doesn't. Trust your emotions and feelings to guide you, not control you.

It takes practice, but we can apply *emotional maturity* to everything we say and do. We choose our emotional response and state of being from the maturity we have now.

A couple of summers ago, I was golfing with an elderly couple. After the game, the wife was bemoaning a shot she had missed. Peter, her husband, said, "Don't look back on your life with regret, or you will die of remorse." That's *emotional maturity*; that's emotional ZEST. He was telling her not to fall into the negative emotion and feelings of regret. She couldn't get the shot back, but she could move on. I'm not convinced that she was really upset about her shot; it was her way of making conversation and asking for attention and external validation.

Creating emotional maturity is the embodiment of love and self-responsibility. Feeling your emotions is important, and you can do so without losing your ZEST, your power, or your energy. Stand strong in your power-filled stories because they influence your emotions positively. Understand the impact of emotional ZEST and the effect you have on others as well. Remember that how you put your energy into the world matters—size matters!

BE AWARE AND IN TUNE WITH HOW YOU FEEL

Contraction and expansion happen all the time. They are happening right now. When we breathe in we expand and we breathe out we contract. We want that expansion and contraction in our breathing, and we also want them in our feelings. What we don't want is to get stuck in either state. We need both to have a healthy flow of energy.

Sometimes feelings may cause you to contract, pull into yourself, and feel that you are imploding. *You don't want to see anyone. You've got a secret. You're anxious, afraid, ashamed, embarrassed, or depressed.* Can you remember times when you got those feelings? Maybe you had to make a decision and you knew that it wasn't the right thing for you, but you went ahead and did it anyway. Every time that I have done that in my life it has turned out badly for me. There were a few years when those lessons came fast and furious. Once in a while, I still screw up by trying to please others or by doing too much and not listening to myself. I know that it is happening because I have that contracted feeling or I get sick.

My decision making works best when I follow the feelings of expansion, love, and joy and go for that. That's a ZEST energy booster because it's in alignment with my authentic self and my purpose. It creates the feeling of being connected to the world, loving others, and knowing that they love me. I sit up straighter and when I stand, I feel taller. It comes when I laugh with a child and achieve a desire. When I make a decision, I know that it's the right thing to do. It's best for me and it's best for those around me too.

Experience what your body feels going on around you. The more often you do this, the easier it is to do it intentionally. Your intuition guides you to be present and alert in every moment. Take the time to examine, process, and understand a situation. Look at it from different points of view and ask questions that lead you to the right decision for every step of your life.

It may seem contradictory, but I know that when I was most miserable I was healing to overcome my perceptions and beliefs regarding my, regrets, what or who hurt me, and what I resented. It took courage to sort out the real truth about the situation and understand what had gone on from the perspective of my woman of power and not from my wounded, contracted ego.

Emotional maturity shortens the recovery time from when you are presented with challenges to when you find your balance of energy. Even in the most challenging situations, you can choose how you react. Now you're the driver in your life—not the passenger being pushed and pulled by emotions. You experience a gain in ZEST energy, and that's nice—very nice.

EMOTIONAL REACTIONS TO PHYSICAL CHANGES

The influx of hormonal changes can be seen in girls from a very early age. Female bodies transform from being a girl to being a woman. Women adapt to change. Every month for many years, female bodies change and flow. Women operate on a cycle of change, even after the blood flow stops. These physical changes are always accompanied by emotional changes.

The beginning and the end of a woman's menstrual cycle are significant passages. They used to be celebrated with sacred rites of passage ceremonies. There are stories told of a time when women retreated to "the red tent" during their menstruation. They supported each other and shared their lives, sorrows, and joys. Women who live together often have synchronized menstrual cycles.

Menstruation may be a time when the veil between the spiritual world and our human world is the thinnest. You may find your connection to your ancestral line provides you with a vision of the patterns in your family relationships and how to change them. Don't dismiss your emotional intelligence. Allow for the deeper truths to come to the surface, and be more receptive.

You are being offered a monthly opportunity to rebirth yourself. Sometimes giving birth is scary, painful, and challenging. Being vulnerable and asking for a midwife is a sign of strength, power, and belief in yourself. Attending another woman's rebirth is one of the great joys that I experience in the work that I do. In doing so, I am rebirthed and no longer the same.

Premenstrual syndrome (PMS) refers to symptoms related to a woman's menstrual cycle. The research into the causes and treatments for PMS are still controversial. Many women experience mild to severe emotional distress and physical discomfort during their menstrual cycles. My advice is to eat well, drink plenty of water, and take extra special care of yourself during this sacred time.

> *"A period of healing from childhood wounds*
> *frequently occurs for women in their mid thirties*
> *and early forties as the profound changes leading*
> *to menopause begin."*
> —*Joan Borysenko*

Undergoing a hysterectomy is a definitive end to child bearing and can trigger menopause and be emotionally traumatic. Menopause with its hot flashes, night sweats, and mood swings can launch you head first into a time of change and turmoil. It may be helpful to think of the hot flashes as your body heating you up to sterilize and eliminate all the badness of the past—to purify you for a future of health and happiness.

This time is an opportunity to change the patterns in your life. My big change was not a conscious one. Menopause left me with a unique effect; I became a clean and neat fanatic. For example, before menopause, I would wash the dishes and pile them sky high to let them air dry. Laundry was washed, but left in the basket and my folding was inadequate when it did get done. Post menopause, I am meticulous about the cleanliness and tidiness of my house and everything in it. The clothes in my drawers are all perfectly folded and sorted. When the mover came to pack our house, she said that she had never seen such a neat and tidy linen closet.

Menopause propels us to *create emotional maturity*. I know many women who have experienced a new mindset toward life after menopause. They have a lower tolerance for bullshit and a greater ability to "let it go." They don't worry so much about the small things in life. They realize that life is too short to spend it in misery, mediocrity, or misunderstanding. The quest is for more ZEST and energy.

Women support each other during these significant changes, and we understand that these life cycles are an integral part of being female. By supporting other women, we bolster the ZEST in our circles of influence and at the same time we sustain our own ZEST.

EMOTIONALLY DISCERNING COMMUNICATION

How you work, live, and play with others is a consequence of how you communicate with those around you. Communicating is an exchange of energy between the speaker and listener. Knowing what provokes different emotions helps you to choose your words carefully, and not to purposely trigger someone else's emotional wounds. Listen past the words to feelings and meaning, as well as what the person is trying to convey to you.

"Within the word 'swords' is the word 'words'.
This is an easy way to remember just what it is that causes or relieves struggle...
Now we are learning that our words, thoughts, and attitudes create our reality of conflict or peace.
Before you learn to take command of your words and the combinations of words that are your beliefs and attitudes, the sword is an appropriate symbol for them.
Your words, like swords, get you into and out of trouble."
—*Carol Bridges, www.EarthNationLifeCeremonies.com*

EMOTIONAL AUTHENTICITY

How do you really feel right now, in this moment—not in your head, but how do you feel in your womb and in your heart? That is emotional authenticity. Occasionally, there are times when I have not been emotionally authentic and it's embarrassing to admit, but I certainly have projected my emotions onto others. It's like the parent yelling at the child who was lost, but has been found.

We all struggle with being able to discern when others are projecting their emotions onto us. It had been many years since someone had yelled at me, and I find it ironic that as I was writing this section of the book, I experienced exactly that—not only once, but three times within a couple of months. All three times I went through a cycle of my energy contracting and then expanding.

Here's the process I went through: I was stunned and silent (contraction), I took a couple of deep breaths, and did a quick review of what I had done to trigger this attack. Then I got out of my head and went into my heart and accepted responsibility. I responded from my heart and a place of love (expansion).

The people I experienced this conflict with were each going through a great deal of pain and sorrow in their lives. I told them that my intent was never to hurt them and I was there for them if they wanted my help. I did not accept the projection of their pain and misery onto me, while at the same time, being emotionally authentic allowed me to stay in my own feelings and emotions.

Think of your authentic self—your higher self—as a favorite teacher or wise fairy godmother. Like your circle of wise women, ask her for help; she's always there for you. Most of us have been taught that wisdom must come from outside of ourselves. Knowledge comes from outside; wisdom comes from inside. It's what you do with your knowledge that turns it into wisdom.

EMOTIONALLY GROUNDED

Sometimes when the contracting or expanding energy whirls, you get lightheaded, and you can't calm down. When this happens put your hands in the earth; if you can't get outside, a flower pot works fine. Breathe fully and feel your body calm right down. This may sound a bit unconventional, but just try it.

WHERE YOU PUT YOUR ENERGY

Where you put your energy makes a big difference to your emotional response. When your energy is in your head, you are thinking of excuses, reasons, or rebuttals. When your energy is in your heart, you can open up to feeling. Trust yourself to take the necessary steps that will get you where you want to be. Instead of struggling and trying to maneuver, be patient and let things be. The path may not be what or how you planned it, but you'll be exactly where you need to be to learn and gain the knowledge that takes you beyond where you ever imagined.

I'm still surprised when this happens. Within one year of creating my ZEST vision board, I bought the house that I now live in. I love the red, terra-cotta, and yellow colors of Arizona and the American southwest. I found a listing for a house that had all these colors. It was a large, older home about a ten minute drive from my daughter's family. It also had a 2.5 million dollar asking price. I like to dream big, so I printed the listing and put it on my vision board.

I didn't get that exact house, but I got a house that is even better. It has all the colors that I love, didn't cost me millions, is only a few years old, is the right size, and it's only four doors away from my daughter and her family. I put my energy into the intent of having the right home.

"Imagination is everything. It is the preview of life's coming attractions."

—*Albert Einstein*

CIRCLE OF CONCERN AND CIRCLE OF INFLUENCE

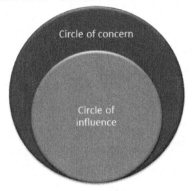

Adapted from The 7 Habits of Highly Effective People by Dr. Stephen R. Covey.

One way to master your emotions and increase your ZEST is to understand the power in the circle of concern and circle of influence. The circle of concern consists of all of the things you are worried or concerned about, but over which you probably have little or no control: war, poverty, the environment, terrorism, and the weather. Within the circle of concern, you have the circle of influence. The circle of influence holds those things you can do something about. You can influence or control them. You have direct control and influence over your own behavior, some aspects of your health, your children (especially if they are young), and/or problems at work.

When you look at the circle of concern and the circle of influence, which of these do you want to invest your energy into?

Is it up to you to make sure all the people in your house have clean socks? I know a woman whose husband often complained that he didn't have any clean socks to workout in because their teenage children always took them. One morning, she intervened when the kids took his socks, and the next thing she knew, they were all yelling at her. From then on, she let them all take responsibility for their own socks.

Do others want you to invest your energy in other people's problems? The only way you know is to ask the direct question. When my son was getting married, he and his fiancé were doing all the planning themselves. They were in their thirties and both very capable of doing it. My husband thought that I should get involved and offer to help. With my husband in the room, I picked up the phone, got them both on the line, and asked: "Would you like me to stick my nose into organizing your wedding?" They both laughed and said they would call when they needed me. And they did call about the wording on the invitation, but that was all.

Others' problems may be in your circle of concern, but not in your circle of influence. They may not want you to "stick your nose in" or be the "sock police."

It's a waste of time to try to manage the socks for a grown man! We want others to respect our boundaries, and we must do the same for others. Respect for socks, clothing, agendas, time, knowledge—all have their own boundaries. Here is the third of *Seven Secrets* that I listed at the beginning of Chapter One...

Secret #3 Women with ZEST manage their time and agendas.

CIRCLES: WHAT GOES WHERE?

The benefit of doing this next exercise is to clearly see what is in your circle of concern and what is in your circle of influence. Identify what you are most emotionally attached to right now and discern if those things give you energy and add to your life—or if they deplete your energy and make you tired.

1. Divide a page into five columns. In the first column, make a list of ten to twelve of your strongest attachments: friends, acquaintances, Facebook friends, colleagues, customers, clients, bosses, pets, animals, your home, your car, clothes, jewelry, toys, and the environment.

2. In the next column beside each item that gives you energy, categorize the energy that each item brings to you. Where an item makes a positive difference or addition to your life, put a plus sign. Next to the ones that make you tired or even grumpy put a minus sign. If you're not sure if an item is a plus or minus, then think about how you would feel if it was not in your life. Would you be happier or distressed and upset?

Circle of Concern/Circle of Influence				
Strongest attachments	Plus or minus in my life	Guilt	Concern	Influence

Keep the list close by; you're going to need it again after reading the next section to complete the remaining columns.

OBJECTS

Many people believe that objects hold the energy of their owner(s) and even the energy of those who made it. It's called the Law of Contagion. Many religions hold the relics of saints and other virtuous people as being sacred. Legends even have been told about using a person's clothing or lock of hair to cast a spell or curse him or her.

Purging or cleansing objects that are sapping your energy and contaminating your emotions is a way of increasing your emotional ZEST. Look around; are you holding onto something that is really not important to you, but was really important to someone you care about? For example, maybe you're keeping your grandmother's dishes, but you never use them and you don't really like them. In fact, if you got rid of them, you could experience a gain in energy. You may even be able to sell them and make good use of the money or donate the money to a cause in your grandmother's name.

Let's keep it simple. If something you have an attachment to makes you feel good, then keep it. However, if something makes you feel bad, then if you can you should get rid of it. Now is the time to eliminate the things that no longer serve you and dispose of the meaningless items in your life. It's time to clean out the clothes that you don't wear. Why are you keeping them? If an item doesn't make you feel great when you wear it then give it away. Someone else may really gain some enjoyment from it. Then:

- Change the energy of items you want to keep. Wash objects in running water, a tap, or a stream; or burn sage and use the smoke to "wash" the items. This changes the energy they hold and emit.

- Set a clear intent of what energy and benefits you would like to gain from each object. A keepsake from a special deceased friend or relative can make you feel closer to the memory of that person.

- To conclude this exercise, look at everything on your list in the previous chart and decide if they belong in your circle of concern or circle of influence. Put a circle around those that you can and want to invest your energy into. Focus more on each one that adds to your energy, love, and happiness. When you are giving from the heart and are not sacrificing yourself negatively, volunteering and helping others adds to these as well.

Affirmation:
I focus on my circle of influence
to make a positive difference.

ENVIRONMENT

Environments can have different emotional effects on people. The environments at home, at work, at a restaurant, or even while shopping, watching movies, listening to stories, or telling stories can all stimulate positive emotional responses. Places, spaces, and environments where you feel safe, comfortable, and appreciated feed and renew your energy. They make you want to spend more time there. They support you, uplift you, and provide comfort and renewal.

I remember walking into the hospital with my sister and as we stepped over the threshold, at the same time we said, "I hate this place." Our father was dying and we had lost our mother at that hospital. A hospital environment can trigger memories of loss and pain for some, but for others it is a place of healing, joy, and new life.

A stage or podium can be terrifying for someone who has a fear of speaking in public or it can be exhilarating for someone who thrives on performing.

Colors in environments have been researched for their impact in schools, hospitals, and retail spaces. The colors of your clothing and your home communicate a message about your taste and personality. Color can affect mood, mental clarity, and energy level.

Alter the environment where you spend the most time to provide you with the mood, mental clarity, and energy level that you seek.

Name three things that you can do immediately to change the environment around yourself so that you gain energy, comfort, and vitality. Take action. Do those things. Will you:

- Tidy up

- Clean up

- Add flowers

- Wash the windows

- Fluff up the pillows

- Move the furniture around

- Cleanse your energetic space with the smoke from burning sage and/or cedar?

- What else?

Do you feel better now?

Affirmation:
My personal effort makes my world a better place.

MONEY

Thoughts about money are wrapped up in many beliefs and emotions. The thoughts about money that is yours, money that is not yours, how much you have, and how much you would like to have all carry emotional charges. The focus and beliefs that you have about money give it the energy and power that it has in your life. Some people believe money is the source of all evil and the other extreme believes it to be the source of all hedonism, pleasure, and satisfaction.

It is really easy to feel depressed and become a victim of not having enough money, especially if you watch television shows about the rich and famous. What your brain sees and hears, it believes. It is not possible for your brain to discern that these stories are deliberately designed and developed to illustrate only the most positive point of view.

Have you been able to overcome believing that money can make you happy or miserable, or that rich people are snobs? Make the necessary changes to align with your values and your beliefs about money. Don't let your thoughts and beliefs hold you back. Clear your thoughts and beliefs by asking the judicious questions from Chapter Three.

Your thoughts about money should fuel your energy—not depress and deplete you. Any negative thoughts block the energy of money and what money can buy from manifesting in your life. Allow positivity and love to flow into your heart so that energy for positive abundance can manifest.

THE EMOTIONAL BANK ACCOUNT

Dr. Stephen R. Covey, author of *The 7 Habits of Highly Effective People*, uses the "emotional bank account" metaphor as a symbol of the amount of trust that has been built up in a relationship. We all know what a financial bank account is. You make deposits into it and then you have a reserve where you can take withdrawals.

The emotional bank account works the same way; there are deposits and withdrawals. For example when you meet someone new and you lend her fifty dollars, if she pays you back promptly and shows appreciation this behavior builds trust. If she doesn't pay you according to your agreement the trust in the relationship is reduced and there is a withdrawal in the emotional bank account.

Another example: if you tell someone a secret, and she doesn't tell anyone, that builds trust deposits in the emotional bank account. Maybe several weeks go by and she still hasn't told anyone your secret. But then after three months you hear that she has told someone. Then the trust that has built up over the months goes down and may even be in a deficit.

The trust level can start high or low.

- Some people start with high trust and then *deduct*. These people trust others the moment they meet them. It's only when someone is rude, discourteous, or deceitful that they reduce their level of trust.

- Some people start with low trust and *build up*. These people have low trust in the people they meet. Everyone must prove themselves and build their level of trust in the relationship.

DEPOSITS AND WITHDRAWALS

Study in your home to see how much negative or positive energy is being exchanged. If you want an interesting experience, listen to conversations in your home. Are people being nice to each other verbally or are they accusing each other, attacking each other, finding fault, and confessing each other's sins endlessly? Often, we take our families for granted and start taking withdrawals from them. We assume that everything's fine. Any close relationship can deteriorate if deposits are not continually made.

On the other hand, if you meet old high school friends, the trust is high because there have been no withdrawals, and the trust that was there years ago still remains. This may be because these relationships were developed during a positive time when life had yet to give you as many battle scars!

Movies and television shows are excellent sources to observe examples of deposits and withdrawals from the emotional bank accounts. There are often more withdrawals than deposits. These stories may be entertaining, but they are not effective examples of how to build relationships in real life.

The key to maintaining positive emotions in relationships is to make deposits—many deposits—and not to get into withdrawal mode. The tendency is to go into withdrawal mode because something happened or was said that triggered you to start withdrawing.

Deposits for Life

"There are two things people want more than sex and money—recognition and praise," said Mary Kay Ash, founder of Mary Kay cosmetics. Recognize when someone makes an effort for you, and thank them. You may not be rewarded with a pink Cadillac like Mary Kay gave to her best sales people, but you'll know that you made a difference. Practice this over the next few days. Take every opportunity to look someone in the eyes and say "thank you". Thank the person who hands you your coffee, opens the door for you, cleans off the table, delivers your mail, or tells you that you look nice. The opportunities to say thank you are boundless. Please post your results on the Facebook group page: ZEST your Life, www. Facebook.com/groups/zestyourlife

"Making deposits" does not mean that you become permissive or soft. That in itself would create a massive withdrawal. It doesn't mean that you abandon all boundaries. I'm talking about building the emotional bank account through making many deposits, so that the trust gets higher and the feeling is good and strong and then you will have a huge reserve. You can make mistakes; those you trust can even correct them. For instance, you probably know people who have such an excellent relationship where the trust is so good that they can make mistakes in communication and they'll still get the meaning. You can even communicate without words, remember? Because the nonverbal communication is so powerful and so real. With those you trust fully, you know each other so well that you often can anticipate each other's intentions and read the real meaning.

Constantly making deposits is the key to maintaining ZEST and positive emotions in relationships—and with your relationship with yourself. When you get yourself into a vicious cycle, stop taking withdrawals and start making deposits. Nothing stops you from making a deposit to yourself. You need to build your trust muscles so that you maintain a strong faith in yourself. Positive self-talk that recognizes your efforts and praises you encourages you to be happy and ZESTY. Try it; you'll be astounded by the results.

Chapter 6
Barriers to Emotional ZEST

*"What we hold in our thoughts, beliefs, and
unresolved emotions
may be the greatest threat to our health in our
lifetime."*
—Dr. Lise Janelle, DC

EMOTIONALITY

Emotionality is reenacting a painful, emotional experience—either real or perceived as real. Did visualizing your father, mother, sibling, or significant other bring up your painful feelings and stories? Are you losing energy by being in *emotionality* right now—by reenacting a painful, emotional experience? Emotionality keeps you spinning the stories instead of moving on. It is the internal dialogue that proves, confirms, and justifies that you are a victim.

When women offer each other empathy they can easily keep the spinning going by telling more and more painful stories about sad, miserable experiences in their lives and the lives of their friends. Although the intent to provide empathy and understanding is good, the result is not. It's really not helpful to keep scratching at the scar, complaining, and blaming others.

We've all been there. Emotionality does not create a position of power. It is a place where you lose energy.

Another example of spinning these painful stories involves *escalating the story*. If you really want something, but don't get it your story may go from not getting this one thing to "I never get what I want", and then you start making a list of all the things you don't have. Doing so only feeds the emotionality. If someone does something and disappoints you, does your story go from the matter at hand to making a list of all the disappointments that can even be remotely related? If so, the process becomes rather irrational and counterproductive to healing.

Have you ever thought yourself into absolute fear; worrying about why someone is late or didn't call, while you make up terrible scenarios until you were almost physically ill? What a waste of energy it is to tell yourself those stories.

When you feel the emotionality starting in your abdomen and moving up to your chest and constricting your throat, breathe into your chest, push the air to your abdomen and to your womb space. Two finger widths below the belly button, inside the body, closer to the spine, is your chi point. Breathing long and deep gives you power and energy by providing more oxygen to the brain.

Your perception of a situation dictates your emotional response. Be aware of the source of your emotionality and choose how you respond. Choose conscious perception, and make your conscious emotional mature response your choice. What is the perspective from the other person's point of view? Stay out of the emotionality drama and don't create it for others.

Eliminating objects that no longer feel good can be cathartic, but seldom can you eliminate people from your life. Casting someone out of your heart and life is seldom a simple, easy decision. You alone can decide what circumstances would merit no longer associating with someone. If eliminating people from your life is not the goal, what can you do to change a relationship to make it more meaningful and nurturing *for you*? What can you do immediately to create happier, deeper relationships with the people in your life? Here are some guidelines and deposits for keeping emotionality out of your relationships:

- Focus more energy into each relationship that adds to your ZEST, your love, and your happiness.

- Focus more energy into adding more care and honor to your relationships.

- Treat others the way you want to be treated.

- Reduce the complaints and the criticism.

- Increase the compliments.

- Be the person you'd want to come home to.

FEAR

Fear is a barrier to emotional ZEST; it can cause an unconscious, immature, and emotional reaction of inappropriate behaviors—like flying into a rage, yelling, throwing a temper tantrum, and all kinds of other nasty things.

"When fear is in control of your life, you're not!"

Fear is a fact of life. Does fear serve you in this moment? If you're running from danger it sometimes does. Often, in looking deeper, you see that it is rooted in an old pattern—which is a barrier holding you back from being your authentic self and creating the life you want.

Understanding your fear increases your belief in yourself, how you judge yourself, and what you think of yourself. When you understand fear in yourself, you can understand fear in others.

Power-filled energy is expressed in words and actions. When you are able to express yourself and contribute to your ZEST, you love yourself more, and you spread that love to everyone who comes near you. You rebuild the self-confidence and self-esteem that were taken from you. You recognize that you are a giver of love and you are able to receive and accept love.

Being afraid to express yourself diminishes you. It is fear that caused your powerful vitality to go underground, to hide, to camouflage itself, to shape shift into sneakiness, depression, and/or complaining. When you are in the emotional state of fear, you are lacking self-confidence and trust in yourself. Fear is based in the future of what terrible thing may happen.

Fear can manifest in many ways; all of them lack personal power. Here are a few examples:

- Fear of failure
- Fear of success
- Fear of being alone
- Fear that being in your power will cause people not to love you
- Fear of speaking out in the face of injustice
- Fear of speaking in public
- Fear of being too analytical
- Fear of not being smart enough
- Fear of being with people or needing people
- Fear of being "too much"
- Fear of being "not enough"

Fear of not being heard may manifest as talking a lot and/or wanting people to hear how smart you are. Strong, confident people don't have to talk a lot to be heard. Are you drawn to someone who talks constantly or are you drawn to someone who talks when he or she has something to say—something that you're interested in? Most likely, you are drawn to people who seem to speak to you and with you, rather than at you.

Fear of power and fear of being powerful can be debilitating. A woman in one my sessions feared the word "power". The examples that she used in her life experiences were negative: a domineering father, then a domineering husband, and a mother who had no power. Professionally, she was successful, but in her family she gave all of her power to others. They made demands of her time and energy. She was frustrated until she came to terms with the fact that she wanted and needed personal power in her life. Then she was able to embrace the power that she had and start putting it into her community and making the world a better place.

Fear can also trigger anger. For example, you're shopping and you can't find your children. When you do find them, you are relieved, but you yell at them. You are angry because you are afraid of what might have happened to them. If you don't have children, you may remember experiencing this when you were a child. Your parents were upset because they were afraid that you were lost.

Change can sometimes pull you off your balance. Sudden change can trigger fear. Does this sound familiar? "Why can't they stick to the plan?" "No one told me things had changed." "When did that happen?" Unexpected change can rock your world.

Consider Julie, who is afraid of speaking in public, and when she is put in those situations she is knocked off balance. When asked for her opinion in a group, Julie is embarrassed and feels singled out. Without adequate preparation time she is afraid of saying the wrong thing, having her colleagues criticize her, and even losing career advancement opportunities. The situation brings her into the past, and she is afraid of stuttering like she did as a child. She is angry because she has not overcome her fear and learned to speak using her personal power.

EXAMPLES OF LIMITING FEARS:

- What are you afraid of? *I am afraid of dogs.*

- Why? What is the cause of your fear? *Because a dog bit me when I was young. My fear is the result of the belief that a dog might bite me.*

- What are you afraid of? *I am afraid of success.*

- Why? What is the cause of your fear? *Because if I'm rich, I won't be a nice person. Because if I'm successful once, I won't be able to keep it up or do it again.* (Fear is the result of the belief that success will have negative consequences.)

It is easy to see from these examples that fear can limit your joy, vibrancy, and happiness.

Take some time to think about the following questions and write down the answers. As you think about your answers, consider how these barriers are preventing you from being a powerful woman and from being as vibrant, happy, and successful as you want to be?

- What situation pulls you off your balance? What situation comes to mind first? What is the cause of this fear?

- What person pulls you off your center? Who pushes your buttons? What is the cause of this fear?

- What are you afraid of? Why? What is the cause of this fear?

- Who are you afraid of? Why? What is the cause of this fear?

In this exercise, did you discover the situations and characteristics in people that present barriers and stop you from being your authentic self? When you are able to find the root cause of your fear you can clear its barriers.

Using the example of Julie, she could respond to publicly posed questions by saying, "I'll need to think about that. I'll get back to you." She could say that she needs time to prepare before she can speak in public. She also could receive training in public speaking to ease her fear. Make your wishes known; it's the only way people around you will know what you want.

Consider it an opportunity for learning if you find that a certain individual or a few individuals pull you off your balance. Why are they in your life? Focus on what you can learn from these experiences. They might be really good examples of what *not* to do and how *not* to behave.

Taking small steps to remove barriers can help you hold onto your ZEST in even the most difficult situations, like the ones you identified in the previous exercise. Do you need to see the situation from the other person's perspective? Others may be going through something personal and their behavior is not about you. In their behavior, they may be trying to hand you the responsibility for their lives. But each person's life is his or her own responsibility. You can't live a life for anyone else and you can't manage it either.

Accept that the situation has happened and then let go of the past that you wanted, but didn't get. I once had a young girl tell me that she wasn't going to speak to her mother again until her mother started being a better parent. I explained that her expectations would never be met because her mother thought that she already was a good parent.

Can you go into your heart and feel some empathy, patience, and understanding for this person? Can you go into your heart and feel some empathy, patience, and understanding for yourself in this situation? Can you see this person and yourself in the light of love? Is it time for forgiveness for both of you?

"Forgiveness is not always easy. At times, it feels more painful than the wound we suffered, to forgive the one that inflicted it. And yet, there is no peace without forgiveness."

—Marianne Williamson

FEELING AND BEHAVING LIKE A VICTIM

Consider the woman who is terrified of speaking in public. Every time she has to speak in front of more than a few people, the memories of painful and terrifying experiences come flooding into her mind. By reenacting the experiences and reliving those feelings, she is in a complete state of fear, emotionality, and victimization. Her behavior is driven by her beliefs that speaking in public is a painful experience. Her behavior may become inappropriate. She doesn't directly say what her problem is; instead she may lash out, yell, and scream at someone about something small and unrelated.

She continues to live the story of how hurtful and humiliating it was as a child to speak with a stutter in public. When she chooses to respond differently and behave differently—by understanding that she is safe and no one will mock or hurt her—she steps out of her fear and emotionality. When she does, *that* is a power story!

When I provide speakers with training and coaching, I tell them what my speaking coach, Steve Lowell told me, "Never bring to the stage a story that you have not yet claimed victory over." When you claim victory over your story, it brings you the confidence to speak about it and not break down. It gives you the confidence of the victorious warrior.

Being excessively sensitive can lead to assuming and jumping to conclusions about something that was said or done. Sometimes it is not even about you; not everything others say or do is about you. Maybe they are having a bad day or maybe they are trying to deal with an illness or difficult relationship, and they are having an "unconscious, immature, emotional reaction".

The twin to being oversensitive is to have no sensitivity to anyone else's feelings. You're so busy thinking about yourself and/or blaming others that there's no time and effort put into how the situation may be affecting others. This is not an uncommon reaction to a crisis, an illness, a death, or a divorce.

Did you come from a dysfunctional family or workplace? Shame and embarrassment are often used by parents, teachers, and bosses. You need to change the belief about what they said and did. Realize that although not long ago their behavior was acceptable, they were wrong to do that.

When you blame others, you are giving away your power and becoming the victim. Look back; what part did you play in your misery? You didn't know any better, so suffering may have been largely of your own making. It may not have been the fault of your husband, your job, or your kids. It's time to stop blaming your parents, your siblings, your teachers, your ex, your boss, etc. Acknowledge and forgive yourself for whatever role you had in your unhappiness.

Go back to your circle of concern/circle of influence. Make a list of everything that you fear and put it in your circle of concern or your circle of influence. In your circle of influence, put fears that are within your power to control, change, or manage. In your circle of concern, put fears that you have no influence or control over.

Now for the tricky one: if the fear lies in your circle of concern and not in your circle of influence then you have no control over it, but it still may be controlling you. What fears are causing you concerns about a situation that you cannot influence? For example, someone close to you may be going through a divorce or illness and you are worried about him or her. The awareness that you are concerned, but cannot influence the situation, may give you some comfort.

We do it all the time, but it doesn't make sense to put energy into worrying about situations or people that are out of your circle of influence. Sometimes all we can do is send them love.

You are not happy when someone or something hijacks your agenda, your time, or your energy. When that is the situation, it can lead to some troublesome behavior; pouting, sulking, and sullenness all come to mind. There is no ZEST in that. You may be able to influence the situation by opening effective communication and making your wishes known.

Shift your mindset out of fear, and open the fear barrier that is blocking your emotional ZEST.

> **Affirmation:**
> **I release my fears. I am safe, and in control of my life.**

ANGER

Anger is a barrier to emotional ZEST.

Here are some wise words from Gregg Braden's book, *Walking Between the Worlds:* "While anger may be a socially acceptable way of responding to an event of horror, ask yourself, 'Does my anger serve me in this moment?' Does the situation warrant your response of emotional contraction, physiological depression, and the compromise of your immune system—each an expression of anger?"

You may feel anger for many different reasons. You may not even know the reason. When you get that tightness and contraction in your body, ask yourself: "Why am I feeling angry right now?" "What is the cause of my anger?" "Am I mad at myself?" "Did I have a bad dream?" Hurt feelings and memories of hurt feelings can be the cause of anger. Memories can be triggered by music, sound, or even smells. Anger is based in the past, whether that past is a far distant memory or an event that happened only moments ago.

Embarrassment or being put down in public or in front of another person can also be the cause of anger. Sometimes anger is used to avoid contact and connection with people—to keep them away and not engage in relationships. Anger can also be a trigger that puts you into action mode and helps you realize that you need to make changes.

Guilt

Guilt is a barrier to emotional ZEST. Guilt is a feeling of having done something wrong or let someone down. You feel guilt and regret for something you have done or not done, said or not said. It could have been an innocent mistake, but guilt carries the feeling of powerlessness and causes nasty behavior such as lashing out.

Guilt can rear its ugly head in the form of accusations. For example, a child accuses her friend of yelling at her and being mean. You may have to ask the child many times what *she* did to her friend, but eventually the answer comes out. "Well, I was hungry, so at recess I took the sandwich out of her lunch and ate it." Of course, the child should think of how she can make this right. She could make her friend a sandwich every day for a week. Even a child understands why her friend was yelling at her and being mean.

Next time you accuse someone of something, verbally or mentally, ask yourself: "What have I done?" "What have I done?" "What have I done?" "What have *I* done?", until you discover the truth. Find your own guilt, shame, and regret. Take responsibility. What action must you now take?

Think about each relationship that you have in your life. Refer to the list you made earlier in Chapter Five, *Circles: What Goes Where?* Beside each, in the Guilt column, add a "G" if you carry any guilt in that relationship. Do you feel guilt for anything you have done or not done, said or not said? Practicing ZESTERS will help you to absolve all relationships of any need for guilt.

WORDS

Words can be a barrier to ZEST. Learn to choose your words wisely. Your words have influence and impact. Stay away from sarcasm; it is inauthentic, cutting, and hurtful.

If people use hurtful words or yell when they speak to you, tell them to stop. It takes courage. The first time you do this, it's really scary. Breathe, stand strong, and change the pattern.

While correcting or disciplining staff or children, stay with the matter at hand, open your heart, and speak from a place of calm compassion and understanding. This doesn't mean being soft; you can be firm without being mean.

By the way, when talking to yourself, stay away from sarcasm, open your heart, and speak from a place of compassion and understanding. We've all heard enough unpleasant words spoken to us, and we should not add to them.

I AM/I SHOULD

Pastor Joel Osteen says, "Whatever follows 'I am' is going to come looking for you."

"I am tired." "I am mad." "I am fed up." "I am excited." "I am happy." "I am doing great things." Does this make you look at your "I am" statement in a different way?

- Complete this sentence: "I am_____."

- Write down first emotion/feeling that comes to mind.

Watch your "I am" statements, and while you're at it, watch your "I should" statements. What do your "I should" statements

---

say? This is important because "I should" can carry guilt and obligation.

- "I should..."

The purpose of this exercise is to clean up your language and expressions to create positive energy and remove another barrier to emotional ZEST.

Choosing how we speak to ourselves is as important as how we speak to others. Putting ourselves down, criticizing ourselves and having negative self talk is a barrier to emotional ZEST. I often hear women talk about all the things that they are not good at doing, especially if they are giving another woman a compliment. "You're so organized; I'm not good at doing that." Too many women call themselves stupid and beat themselves up.

I once asked a woman who worked at a woman's shelter if she was against violence against women. She replied, "Of course."

I told her, "Then stop beating the shit out of yourself. Be as nice to yourself as you are to me."

You are now awake to what emotionality is and how fear, anger, and guilt can hold you back from achieving your dreams and desires. The barriers to emotional ZEST are not insurmountable. If you do nothing else and read no further, removing the barriers to emotional ZEST changes your life.

Affirmation:
My courageous heart speaks from a
place of love, compassion, and understanding.

Chapter 7
Emotional Masks

An emotional mask is a personality layer that you developed to survive in your environment. Masks were unconsciously created from your experiences and donned as a coping mechanism to protect you from what you perceived as a hostile environment.

Words you have heard and spoken have left wounds. In fact, researchers have studied the importance of words and their impact on water. This is important because up to 60 percent of the human body is water, and 75 percent of the human brain is water. It is not a stretch to conclude that words have an impact on the body.

In the seminal work by Dr. Masuro Emoto, *Messages from Water* (Hay House, 2010), he showed in photographs that "thank you" and words of "love" and "gratitude" produce a vibration that has an effect on the molecular structure of water and creates a hexagon shape in ice crystals. He says, "This principle is what I think makes swearing and slang words destructive. These words are not in accordance with the laws of nature. So, for example, I think you would probably find higher rates of violent crime in areas where a lot of negative language is being used."

As a tiny baby you didn't wear a mask, but it didn't take long before you learned that you were no longer totally free to be who and what you really were. Like the water, you learned to differentiate soothing, safe sounds from harsh, dangerous ones. Emotional wounding and/or trauma caused you to put on a mask to protect yourself. Afraid, doubting yourself, and believing that you're not good enough was fertile ground for creating a mask to hide and keep your authentic self safe. You altered your behavior to comply with the persona that you thought your image makers wanted to see.

Masks become a heavy coat of armor, and even though they keep you safe, they rub and chafe against your authentic, ZESTY, power-filled woman. Masks are easily recognizable because they are painful stories that are repeated over and over again. Eventually, you believe them.

Antibiotics kill the bad germs that are in your body that make you sick, but they also kill the good bacteria that we need to be healthy. When you shield anything out by wearing a mask, you shield everything out.

This protective behavior remains as a habit long after you have consciously forgotten where and how it started, when the masks no longer serve you, deplete your energy, compromise your immune system, and make you sick.

You recognize the masks that you wear because all masks feel bad. Masks carry heavy, negative energy, and sad stories from the past.

Here are some examples of masks and stories we tell:

- The "I was adopted" mask.
- The "I grew up poor" mask.
- The "I'm too busy" mask.
- The "I don't have any money" mask.
- The "I'm too tired" mask.
- The "shame" mask.
- The "renegade or rebel" mask. "You can't make me!"
- The "approval" mask—either wanting approval or insisting on giving approval, or refusing approval. "You can't do that without my say so."

- The "people pleasing" mask.

- The "I'm invisible, I don't want to be seen" mask.

- The "perfectionist" mask.

- The "body image" mask. It has several versions: "I'm too fat"; "my boobs aren't big enough"; "my boobs are too big"; "my butt is too big"; "I have no butt"; "my legs are too skinny"; "I have cankles"; "my nose is too big." It goes on and on.

- The "I don't know" mask, to avoid responsibility.

- The "my mother tried to abort me" mask.

- The "my mother/father abandoned me" mask.

- The "my mother/father doesn't love me" mask.

- The "I'm old" mask.

- The "it's not my fault" mask.

- The "but I help people" mask. This is a great mask if you like to stick your nose in other people's business.

- The "I'm emotional because I care too much" mask. Mother Teresa cared, and she didn't stop to cry much.

- The "blame" mask.

- The "I'm sweet" mask.

MASK DANCE

When you tell a story with any of these labels you are putting on a different mask and engaging in the "mask dance". You may not even be aware that you're in the mask dance. You run into someone who hurt you and those feelings well up inside. If you had a pattern of being sarcastic with this person, your old pattern of sarcasm comes back, even though it is not the way you behave now. If you encounter a former partner or spouse, you may wear any of a number of masks: shame, blame, compliance, or sweetness.

MASKS SHOW AND TELL

Masks are heavy, negative, fearful blocks that clog the energy flow. They can be so fused that you don't even realize that they are masks or you justify them. Have you ever heard any of these? "That's the way I am." "I was born this way." "I'm not a morning person." This rigid, dogmatic thinking is mistaking your masks for your authentic self. Just because it is a mask, meaning it is not your authentic self, does not mean that it is not real. It is as real as the mask that a raccoon wears!

Masks communicate what you believe about yourself and/or what you want others to believe about you. They hide your authentic self because you believe you are not worthy of being seen or heard.

Photo by www.JonBabulicPhotography.com

This is an example of a mask that Sue, one of my clients made. Note: for a colored version of this mask go to: www.ZESTyourLife.com/extras

There are two sides to the masks. What you see from the inside looking out is not what others see from the outside looking at you.

Sue describes herself as clever, a quick thinker, a problem solver, and able to devise new and innovative ways to get something done. The mask and its markings were made on the subconscious mind level and at the time she was not aware of all the meanings she had included. She took time, courage, and patience to achieve the level of diagnosis that follows.

On the outside of the mask, the frown and furrow of the brows with lots of patterns on the forehead indicate lots of thinking. The circles around the eyes are black and white, which indicates she wants to show the world that she has no doubt that she has the right answers. She runs circles around her problems. The attention to detail is apparent in all the little circle dots, reminiscent of the phases of the moon. Her knowledge of astrology is further illustrated on each cheek through a planet with rings on the right and an asteroid on the left.

The lines coming down the nose give the impression of a warrior ready to do battle. Notice the ears that are always listening. Nothing gets past her. She seeks the opportunity to get into a conversation and be the center of attention to show everyone that she's smart. Her sharp, quick replies intimidate and hold people away. "Show off the brain and then you won't look for the heart," could be her motto.

At what expense? On the inside, there is a very different story: she is ruthless to herself. The inside of a mask represents what you do to your-self—unconsciously. She never gives herself a break and never lets herself off the hook. She sees things in black and white, as illustrated in the black thought line on the brow and the black lines around the eyes.

The straight red line of responsibility (or what she perceives as her responsibility and within her circle of influence) goes through the jaws of the shark on the forehead. The shark is also present with its sharp fins, sharp tail, and sharp teeth—to lock the jaw into the problem and not let go until it is pulverized.

She is harsh with herself—with intense personal judgment of herself.

She stews over something until she feels it is resolved to her satisfaction, and that may mean stewing for a long time. Someone who is ruthless on the inside can't let go. She deals with the problem, but at what price to herself? Her friends may get tired of hearing about the problem articulated again and again from her many, many different perspectives. She expends a great deal of energy that could be better put to another use. Recall that on the outside, this was expressed as: "She runs circles around her problem."

The woman whose physical mask I just described realized that when she spoke, no one challenged her. Others thought of her as being smart and they were intimidated by her cunning, deviousness, and sneakiness. She sought and enjoyed intelligent and articulate conversation more than most people I know. When she sought the opinion of others, their defensive response was: "I'm not as smart as you. I don't know." She had to relearn to communicate in a way that encouraged dialogue. She had to let go of the fear and start to believe that she was safe in expressing who she was and allow others to freely express who they were.

In her words: "There is no role to play. Now I'm easier on myself and no longer fear that someone will discover that I am not perfect. I believe in myself and believe that I am a good person. My behavior reflects that. I know that not everyone likes me, and I don't like everybody, and I'm good with that."

Her advice: "Build authenticity from a place of knowledge and understanding of why you behave the way you do."

Masks Built on Beliefs

> "Understanding why an emotion is so intense often
> yields an important insight into our psyche."
> —Tara Bennett-Goleman

At this point, you may be asking yourself: "What is the point of exploring the masks?" Pain and sorrow show us the way to healing and open the landscape of our hearts to love and pleasure. Where and when it hurts points us to how it needs healing.

Learn to recognize the patterns of your own behavior and the behavior of those around you. For example, every time her in-laws were coming for a visit, the woman from the mask example would get uptight, bitchy, demanding, and exacting. She was a fanatic about having the house spotless and the meals perfect. This pattern of behavior was ingrained at a very young age, when she saw her father criticize and bully her mother as his family was coming to visit. The mask of perfection was created to hide the fear of being criticized and ridiculed.

An emotional mask is a personality layer that you developed to survive in your environment. It was unconsciously created from your experiences as a coping mechanism to protect yourself from what you perceived as a hostile environment. You put on a mask to keep yourself safe when you believed that you needed to protect yourself.

All behavior is belief driven. You believe something because you think it is true, otherwise you would not believe it. But, is it really true?

You accept the belief that your world is not safe and you behave accordingly. When you believe that you cannot change the life that you have then your behavior and every action that you take reflect this limiting belief. Your beliefs are founded on your experiences.

Your feelings and emotions are the most powerful things you have to help you navigate life. Feelings, thoughts, and beliefs can all be changed. There was a time when people generally believed that their "lots in life" could not be changed—that they had to "play the hands they were dealt." Today, rags-to-riches stories tell us: "If they can do it, I can do it." Oprah, Madonna, and Lady Gaga all have power stories clearly demonstrating that you can change your life from having very little to having a life of abundance.

When you realize that you can change your life, you have the key to create a new belief and story for yourself. The first step is to be aware of the experiences that created your beliefs, maintained your masks, and affected your behavior. Uncover your limiting beliefs, and transform them to work in your favor. Then the masks that are hiding your beauty and shining will dissolve.

I'd like to explore a personal example of how easy it is to change your feelings and your beliefs. In this case, my change was triggered by my daughter. One snowy winter day, my daughter called from Ottawa, five hours away. I complained: "It's snowing like crazy again!"

She responded: "It must be beautiful; I wish I was there." Immediately, I shifted my belief that the snow was a bad thing and my anger changed to happiness because I was safe, warm, and snowbound in my house. I lived in a stunningly beautiful forest.

You must change your beliefs to remove your masks; otherwise, nothing changes. Beliefs are created by your thoughts. To find your beliefs, start with your feelings; they lead you to your thoughts.

For instance, when children are bitten by a dog, they may attempt to avoid all dogs. For some, raising a dog from the time it is a puppy could help eliminate the belief that all dogs bite. There may be other opportunities to be exposed to dogs in a safe environment. I'm not saying that you should go out and buy a puppy, but you get my point.

A belief that horses will harm you can be modified. There are many horse therapy counselors that provide an opportunity to release beliefs and fears about horses. Horses are large creatures and caution around horses is wise. The point in this example is to be sure to talk about the incidents that caused your fears as you then have the opportunity to work through them.

Changes become real when behaviors change and you feel an increase in ZEST energy.

REMOVE THE MASKS

It is time to remove the masks because keeping masks takes a lot of energy. If you continue to live an inauthentic life, you will be unhappy, sad, and unfulfilled. You may even get sick or develop an illness.

Everything starts in the emotional body and it can then manifest in the physical body. If you need proof of this, think about a time when you were given bad news. First your feelings were upset, then you felt it in your body, possibly by crying, shaking, or both. Has witnessing a car accident or something horrible ever made you nauseous?

The process of removing masks helps us to examine beliefs and undo many of the stories that are created through life experiences. It also helps to avoid creating unnecessary new masks.

You can change your beliefs, your thoughts, and your life. The masks change into ZEST as you change what you believe.

> *"Your beliefs become your thoughts,*
> *Your thoughts become your words,*
> *Your words become your actions,*
> *Your actions become your habits,*
> *Your habits become your values,*
> *Your values become your destiny."*
> —*Mahatma Gandhi*

You can say that you think positively all the time, but how you really feel is where the energy comes from. All change needs energy. Mask removal is not for the faint of heart or the impatient. You need truth, courage, and patience. It is a process. Be kind, gentle, and loving to yourself, as well as to each person you interact with during this process.

Fear, grief, pain, anger, terror, loneliness, abandonment, and being a victim are all built on your beliefs and stories. The masks were built on emotions that you believed were true at the time.

Some of them are true, but like a witness at a crime scene, they are not 100 percent reliable. Allow for the possibility that you may not be not witnessing your stories with 100 percent accuracy.

For example, I carried an emotional mask about my mother's death. My mother died when I was seventeen years old; she was forty-seven. For more than thirty-five years, I believed that my mother had abandoned me. In 2005, my close friend committed suicide; she was bipolar. At the memorial, someone said, "She abandoned us."

Suddenly, I had a moment of clarity. My response was: "No, she didn't abandon us; she died." In that instant, I realized that my mother did not abandon me; she simply died. For more than thirty-five years, I had carried the hurt and pain of being abandoned. Suddenly, the burden was lifted. I know that sounds simple, but it was one of those huge insights. I understood that my friend didn't abandon me, and neither did my mother. Newsflash—it wasn't all about me!

This was my greatest mask. It was built by me and based on a story I believed to be true.

YOUR GREATEST MASK

"The truth will set you free,
but first it will piss you off."
—Gloria Steinem

This exercise is to discover your greatest emotional mask, as well as the beliefs and thoughts associated with it. Remember to

---

breathe. Take your time. Take deep breaths as you do this. Focus on the facts and don't traumatize yourself again. My hope is that you have been reading this book with a trusted friend or group of friends and you can do this exercise together. The alternative is to do the telling part of the exercise out loud by yourself. The rest of the answers should be written.

Follow these steps:

- Tell the greatest sad story in your life. Use only the facts. Take only five minutes. You'll know you're finished when you start repeating yourself.

- How does it feel now, in this moment? What are you thinking about that is causing these feelings?

- What is the belief behind these feelings? Where and how did you acquire it?

- With what you know about the situation, is this belief true? Ask yourself again: "Am I sure it's true?" You may do some research by asking others who were there—family members and witnesses. But trust yourself to discern the truth. "With what I know about the situation, is this true? Is it true now?"

- Have your thoughts changed how you feel about it?

- If you can, tell it again, and make it as light as you can.

It can be a tough story, but it doesn't need to hold the emotional charge that it once did. What else do you need to do to make this story simply a story and not a tyrant in your life? If you ever tell this story again, how can you tell it differently?

We develop masks to protect ourselves from traumatic experiences in life. As women, we adapt, change, and transform our entire lives. When we are strong, we find that we no longer need the masks and we can shed them. Even the woman who spent years telling the story of how her mother had tried to kill her removed that painful mask and can stand in her own power.

Every time a woman heals and removes a mask, we are all stronger, and we feel an increase of ZEST energy. Our masks and challenges are not isolated. "Rather, they are staked up like rows of dominoes. If we topple one domino by meeting one challenge plenty of others will follow suit. The results are a feedback loop of positive gain" (Diamandis and Kotler, 15).

Affirmation:
My authentic self dances and
laughs with my face in the sun.

CHAPTER 8
APPLYING THE CHANGE

"18, 40, 60 rule

When you're eighteen, you worry about what
everybody is thinking of you; when you're forty,
you don't give a rip about what anybody thinks of
you; when you're sixty, you realize nobody's been
thinking about you at all."

—*Dr. Daniel Amen*

Emotional ZEST comes about when you are:

- Aware and in tune with how you feel.

- Sensing emotional reactions to physical changes.

- Knowing what words provoke different emotions.

- Able to move from low to high measure.

Secret #4 Consciously directing thoughts and feelings.

Let's examine each of these to help apply the changes that you want
in your life:

Aware and in tune with how you feel. You can't change your feelings
until you become aware of them. The other day I overheard someone say,

"I have to go grocery shopping. I really hate grocery shopping." Hearing what she said shifted me from my happy place to feeling disgusted and even mad at her for leaking her negative energy all over the place. She was hating grocery shopping and I was hating that she said it. Do you think that is a good use of emotional energy?

Sense physical reactions to emotional changes. Be aware of when your voice pitch or volume goes up and check what you are feeling in that moment. It could be a sign that you are nervous or excited. I bite my lip when I'm nervous—this an "emotional tell". Once you identify the feeling then you can change it. Find your voice in a tender moment of affection and use that voice. Make your voice calm, soft, strong, humble, confident, and attentive.

Know what words provoke different emotions. Replace painful stories and memories with a happy ones, like children laughing, birds singing, whatever works for you. Laughter is great for the emotions and the spirit. Turn a frown upside down. Change a miserable snow fall into a winter wonderland of beauty and peace.

Consciously direct thoughts and feeling. Understand the impact of having emotional ZEST and discern where to put your energy. Emotional ZEST is about your own emotions, of course, but think about what is around you. Our purpose as humans is to fully participate in life. You were born with a purpose and that is to love and live in beauty. Tap into your higher purpose and express your gifts to the world. Whenever others ask you how to do something or for advice they are tapping into your gifts. Let's harvest some right now.

YOUR GIFTS

Write down five or more skills, talents, or gifts that you can share with others.

1.

2.

3.

4.

5.

You have been hiding your love, light, and beauty for long enough. The more you give, the more you get. Giving a compliment is an easy way of sharing your gifts and exponentially duplicating their ZEST. Tell others about the ZEST you see in them and the gifts you see that they have.

Affirmation:
I am grateful that I have gifts to share.

"Nobody has ever measured, not even poets, how much the human heart can hold."
—*Zelda Fitzgerald*

STORYTELLING

When we gather with family and friends, often one of the favorite things to do is to tell stories. There is great value in storytelling. It gives us a sense of where we are and where we belong in the family, amongst our friends, and even in history. I take great pride in the fact that my ancestors were amongst the first families to arrive in Canada from France in 1680.

Our lives are filled with stories that make us laugh or cry, but mostly they help us to understand our beliefs and thoughts. We have stories that we tell ourselves and others about how and why our lives are the way they are.

Sometimes these stories and telling them amongst family can help us unravel emotions. For example, your big sister can help you understand why you have a fear of bears. Maybe you didn't know that when you were little you went to a bear show and the handler was poking the bear to make him growl.

In Chapter Five, *Circles: What Goes Where?,* you made a list of your fears and put them in your circle of concern or circle of influence. Please refer to that list now.

- What stories do you associate with those fears? Make a list of the stories you tell yourself and others about how and why your life is the way it is. These stories contain all of your problems, worries, and concerns—all the pain and despair you have felt. Everything you have seen, heard, and experienced has had an impact on you and shaped who you are.

Listen to your heart. If something hurts then it needs healing. Open your heart to heal the pain and to remember who you really are. Open your heart and become sensitive, but not wimpy. Think about what you are feeling; become aware of your emotions.

Don't give up; these fears and stories hold the beliefs that created the masks you want to get rid of. Remove the masks now. You don't want to be haunted by unrealized dreams and regrets.

- Fill in the blanks for each mask and belief.

    I could have…, but…

    I should have…, but…

    I would have…, but…

- Burn the list and release your painful stories. Removing even one mask frees your mind and emotions. The burden is finally gone. You can now face similar situations with confidence and ease without being pulled back into the cycle of emotionality. Emotional Maturity show us how to understand our painful stories, learn any lessons that might be in them, and dissolve the masks and barriers that no longer serve us. We can trust our intuition and be guided by our emotions instead of being controlled by them.

Affirmation:
I am aware and in tune with how I feel.

"Let everything happen to you
Beauty and terror
Just keep going
No feeling is final"
—*Rainer Maria Rilke*

CREATE EMOTIONAL MATURITY REVIEW

Before you go on, it may be helpful to review the concepts of emotional ZEST to ensure that they stick. This chapter is designed to provide you with a simple overview while exploring some new stories and examples.

Trust your emotions and feelings to guide you, not control you. Ask yourself: "How do I choose to feel right now?" "What do I feel right now?" You can choose your emotional response and state of being from the maturity you have now—thus displaying emotional maturity in everything you think, say, and do. There is no whining or complaining.

EMOTIONALLY DISCERNING COMMUNICATION

In how you work, live, and play with others, choose your words carefully so as not to trigger someone else's emotional wounds. Within the word sword is the word "word." Swords and words can be used for good.

Listen carefully to the meaning of what someone is speaking to you. Don't assume and don't jump to conclusions. Communication is a process whereby messages are sent and received from one person to another. Messages contain two parts: factual content and personal emotion. Words can be heard and actions seen, but you can only infer what these words and actions mean. Emotions and thoughts are often kept private and hidden. However, clues to feelings can be found in behaviors if you probe to uncover them.

Good listeners pay attention to what is said and how it is said. They watch for the non-verbal message and read "between the lines" to seek support for or contradictions to the verbal message.

Staying objective, distinguishing our own projections, and not being triggered into an emotional response takes focus and practice. It helps when you open your heart and surround yourself with love.

EMOTIONALLY AUTHENTIC

How do you really feel right now, in the moment? Not off the top of your head, but how do you feel in your heart?

EMOTIONALLY GROUNDED

Breathing fully, feel your body.

STANDING STRONG IN YOUR POWER-FILLED ZEST STORIES

BE. Be the real you, not the you that you "should be", "could be," or "would be"—and maybe not the you who you have been showing everyone else, if that has not been authentic. When you do this, the mind automatically gets quiet, the itty-bitty-shitty-committee goes on vacation, and the inner dialogue takes a break.

Before you go on to the next chapter, close your eyes. Go back to your favorite lake. The water is calm, the sun is shining, and there is no one around. You walk into the water a little way. As you gaze into the water, you see an image of yourself.

What do you see when you look at yourself? What feelings do you have? Give yourself a big smile filled with love.

CHAPTER 9
PART 2 ZESTERS

Practice these ZESTERS to anchor and reinforce Emotional Maturity.

- Love Yourself. Close your eyes, go inside, and see yourself as your own lover. Feel the love flooding your heart. Let's give that feeling the symbol of a heart; when you see a heart anywhere and anytime, you remember this feeling. Every time you see one, say: "I love you, (insert your name). You are loved." Feel it. Make every heart that you see your heart and feel the love.

- Mindful Bathing. In the morning, when you take your shower or bath, stop planning the day and feel the water on your skin. Breathe the scent of the soap and take that moment to enjoy the experience. Gather the strength and power of the water and your breath to fuel your day with ZEST.

- Try Blissful Bathing. In the evening, take a bath, relax, feel the pleasure of water on your skin, breathe the scent of the soap, and take that moment to enjoy. Gather the strength and power of the water and your breath to fuel your sleep and your dreams.

- Continue to Be in Awareness and Practice Being in Your ZEST. Emotional Maturity gives you the power to be a happier person by shifting how you view the world. Happiness is a learned behavior; you may have to work on it. Many people have never been happy, so they don't know how. The only way you recognize your happiness is by getting in touch with your feelings. Pay attention when you feel happy and notice when you feel sad. Acknowledge your feelings. How does your body feel? Are you standing or sitting a little straighter?

- Cry When You Need to. Crying is a physical expression of your emotions and feelings. Cry when you're happy and cry when you're sad. Dr. Clarissa Pinkola Estes, author of Women Who Run With the Wolves, says: "I am amazed how little women cry nowadays, and then apologetically. I worry when shame or disuse begins to steal away a natural function."

- Write a Contract with Yourself. Here is an example:

Every day, I love myself and tell myself: "(Insert your name), I love you."

Every day, I treat myself with respect.

Every day, I look in the mirror and smile.

Every day, I…

- Forgive Yourself and Others. Let it go. Forgiveness is an act of grace. Dr. Joe Vitale has made Hoʻoponopono (ho-o-pono-pono), the ancient Hawaiian practice of reconciliation and forgiveness popular lately.

THE WORLD'S MOST UNUSUAL THERAPIST BY DR. JOE VITALE

Two years ago, I heard about a therapist in Hawaii who cured a complete ward of criminally insane patients without ever seeing any of them. The psychologist would study an inmate's chart and then look within himself to see how he created that person's illness. As he improved himself, the patient improved.

When I first heard this story, I thought it was an urban legend. How could anyone heal anyone else by healing himself? How could even the best self-improvement master cure the criminally insane?

It didn't make any sense and it wasn't logical. So I dismissed the story.

However, I heard it again a year later. I heard that the therapist had used a Hawaiian healing process called ho'oponopono. I had never heard of it, yet I couldn't let it leave my mind. If the story was at all true, I had to know more.

I had always understood "total responsibility" to mean that I am responsible for what I think and do. Beyond that, it's out of my hands. I think that most people think of total responsibility that way. We're responsible for what we do, not what anyone else does. The Hawaiian therapist who healed those mentally ill people would teach me an advanced new perspective about total responsibility.

His name is Dr. Ihaleakala Hew Len. We probably spent an hour talking on our first phone call. I asked him to tell me the complete story of his work as a therapist. He explained that he worked at Hawaii State Hospital for four years. That ward where they kept the criminally insane was dangerous. Psychologists quit on a monthly basis. The staff called in sick a lot or simply quit. People would walk through that ward with their backs against the wall, afraid of being attacked by patients. It was not a pleasant place to live, work, or visit.

Dr. Len told me that he never saw patients. He agreed to have an office and to review their files. While he looked at those files, he would work on himself. As he worked on himself, patients began to heal.

"After a few months, patients that had to be shackled were being allowed to walk freely," he told me. "Others who had to be heavily medicated were getting off their medications. And those who had no chance of ever being released were being freed."

I was in awe.

"Not only that," he went on, "but the staff began to enjoy coming to work. Absenteeism and turnover disappeared. We ended up with more staff than we needed because patients were being released and all the staff was showing up to work. Today that ward is closed."

This is where I had to ask the million dollar question: "What were you doing within yourself that caused those people to change?"

"I was simply healing the part of me that created them," he said.

I didn't understand.

Dr. Len explained that total responsibility for your life means that everything in your life is your responsibility simply because it is in your life. In a literal sense, the entire world is your creation.

Whew. This is tough to swallow. Being responsible for what I say or do is one thing. Being responsible for what everyone in my life says or does is quite another. Yet, the truth is this: if you take complete responsibility for your life, then everything you see, hear, taste, touch, or in any way experience is your responsibility because it is in your life.

This means that terrorist activity, the president, the economy—anything you experience and don't like—is up for you to heal. They don't exist, in a manner of speaking, except as projections from inside you. The problem isn't with them, it's with you and to change them, you have to change yourself.

I know this is tough to grasp, let alone accept or actually live. Blame is far easier than total responsibility, but as I spoke with Dr. Len, I began to realize that healing for him and in ho'oponopono means loving yourself. If you want to improve your life, you have to heal your life. If you want to cure anyone, even a mentally ill criminal, you do it by healing you.

I asked Dr. Len how he went about healing himself. What was he doing, exactly, when he looked at those patients' files?

"I just kept saying, 'I'm sorry' and 'I love you' over and over again," he explained.

That's it?

That's it.

Turns out that loving yourself is the greatest way to improve yourself and as you improve yourself, you improve your world.

Let me give you a quick example of how this works. One day someone sent me an email that upset me. In the past, I would have handled it by working on my emotional hot buttons or by trying to reason with the person who sent the nasty message. This time, I decided to try Dr. Len's method. I kept silently saying, "I'm sorry" and "I love you," I didn't say it to anyone in particular. I was simply evoking the spirit of love to heal within me what was creating the outer circumstance.

Within an hour I got an e-mail from the same person. He apologized for his previous message. Keep in mind that I didn't take any outward action to get that apology. I didn't even write him back. Yet, by saying "I love you," I somehow healed within me what was creating him.

I later attended a hoʻoponopono workshop run by Dr. Len. He's now seventy years old, considered a grandfatherly shaman, and is somewhat reclusive. He praised my book, *The Attractor Factor*. He told me that as I improve myself, my book's vibration will raise, and everyone will feel it when they read it. In short, as I improve, my readers will improve.

"What about the books that are already sold and out there?" I asked.

"They aren't out there," he explained, once again blowing my mind with his mystic wisdom. "They are still in you."

In short, there is no "out there".

It would take a whole book to explain this advanced technique with the depth it deserves. Suffice it to say that whenever you want to improve anything in your life, there's only one place to look: inside you.

"When you look, do it with love."

This article is from the book *Zero Limits* by Dr. Joe Vitale and Dr. Len."

Affirmation:

**I speak the words of reconciliation and forgiveness.
"I love you. I'm sorry. Please forgive me. Thank you."
This is hoʻoponopono.**

CALL TO ACTION

Choose a few Part 2—ZESTERS that you can implement today. Complete this sentence: I trust my emotions to guide my ZEST by taking action and doing the following:_____

1.

2.

3.

Congratulations! You have created the emotional maturity to lead the rest of your life with less pain, fear, and anger. You understand what to keep in your circle of concern to release the masks that no longer serve you. It's simple: you become happier and happier every day.

PART 3

CONNECT MIND/BODY

The mind/body connection denotes the interdependence, influence, and communication that the mind and body have on each other. It is almost impossible to separate the mind and body from one another. Indeed, without the mind, the body does not function and without a body, there is no mind.

> *"People who experience warm, upbeat emotions*
> *live longer and healthier lives."*
> —*Bethany Kok and Kimberly A. Coffey*

Chapter 10
Mind/Body Research

In his book, *Spontaneous Healing*, Andrew Weil, MD, has this to say about the mind/body connection,

> I see a clear role of the mind in healing; it is visible in correlations of healing responses with mental and emotional changes. For example, a healing response may immediately follow the resolution of some intolerable situation, such as ending a bad marriage, quitting a miserable job, or making peace with an estranged family member. A colleague wrote me that the most dramatic case of healing he has seen was "a bank president with chronic hypertension, whose blood pressure normalized one day after his wife filed for divorce. It dropped to 120/80 and stayed there."

Her blood pressure may have improved too! Dr. Weil goes on to say,

> Another correlation is disappearance of a serious medical problem with falling in love. I have seen this with autoimmunity—rheumatoid arthritis and lupus particularly—and also with chronic musculoskeletal pain and chronic fatigue. I wish I could arrange for patients to fall in love more often.

> *"Love cures all. If it isn't working—double the dose!"*
> —*Anonymous*

The "Feel Good" Hormone

Your mind remembers everything it has ever felt, seen, done, heard, or experienced and your body remembers it all too. Researchers are studying how the entire body holds the memories and how organ recipients acquire some of the cravings and memories of their donors (cellular memory theory). Consider this excerpt from the jacket cover of *A Change of Heart,* by Claire Sylvia:

> After a heart and lung transplant operation, dancer Claire Sylvia discovered that new organs were not the only thing she inherited. Never having liked such foods as beer and chicken nuggets, she suddenly started craving them. After an extraordinary dream, she seeks out the family of her donor—a teenaged boy who died in a motorcycle accident—and learns that it is indeed possible for two souls to merge in one body.

It certainly stands to reason that memories, the associated beliefs, and your behavior affect your body. These can make us feel good - releasing oxytocin - or they can make us feel bad - releasing cortisol (the stress hormone).

Relax and take some deep breaths. What do you feel? Now put your hand on your heart. What do you feel? The mere act of putting your hand on your heart releases oxytocin to your brain.

Oxytocin is the "feel good" hormone; it is reputed to increase mother-child bonding. I wonder if doing this exercise increases the bonding to ourselves? I wonder if that's why in some countries people place their hands on their hearts during the playing of the national anthem?

In the end of Chapter Six, the purpose of the "I am" and "I should" statements was to clean up our language and expressions to create positive energy. Dr. Dan Siegel says, "Consider the difference between saying 'I am sad' and 'I feel sad.' Similar as those two statements may seem, there is actually a profound difference between them. 'I am sad' is a kind of self-definition and a very limiting one. 'I feel sad' suggests the ability to recognize and acknowledge a feeling, without being consumed by it." Feelings are constantly changing.

CREATING UPLIFTING EMOTIONS

Go back to your answers in the "Words" section at the end of Chapter Six, and as you read the statements and hear them, pay attention to how your body feels and changes in only a few moments. "I am tired." "I am mad." "I am fed up." "I am excited." "I am happy." "I am doing great things." How many uplifting "I am" statements can you list?

Breathing with your hand on your heart shows you how to feel the mind/body connection. It clearly illustrates how the mind/body connection is the interdependence, influence, and communication that the mind and the body have on each other.

Affirmation:
I choose and express my words from a center of love and positive intention.

When emotional ZEST is at high measure, it becomes much easier to have mind/body ZEST at high measure as well. Understanding the mind/body connection gives you the ability to respond in a "response-ability" type of way for emotional, mental, physical, spiritual, and sexual health.

Your judgment, criticism, and opinion about your life have an impact on your body and your mind. If you believe that you are a victim of circumstance and you can do nothing about your life situation, then your life manifests around this belief. We have already talked about beliefs and now we can see how the body is also affected by beliefs held in the mind.

VISUALIZATION

Close your eyes and visualize an apple. What color is your apple? See the shine in the skin and its subtle aroma. Visualize that you're eating this apple. Bite into the flesh and feel the juice invade your mouth and the flavor engulf your senses. Feel the changes in your body.

In this exercise, you experienced the impact of visualization from the mental aspect to the changes it created in your body. Your visualization is so powerful that you felt like you just tasted an apple.

Affirmation:
I have a strong mind, and I visualize a life of joy, vibrancy, and ZEST!

THE MIND/BODY WELL-BEING CHECKLIST

The checklist provides you with a quick and easy tool to rate your mind, body, and mind/body.

Use the past six months as your timeline for this exercise. In the space provided, give yourself a rating of between 0 and 10: 0 = never, 5 = sometimes, 10 = full compliance.

1_____ Are you eating good, natural food?

2_____ Are you staying away from filling yourself with empty calories? Junk food?

3_____ Do you stay away from SNACC—sugar, nicotine, alcohol (not a health food), caffeine (dehydrates, constricts blood, increases cortisol = belly fat and sleep interruption), and chemicals (recreational drugs, prescription drugs, toxins in the home and/or workplace)?

4_____ Do you drink eight glasses of water per day? Drink them with gratitude.

5_____ Do you exercise at least three times per week? Move, dance, walk, golf, ski, skate…

6_____ Are you getting rest/quiet time? Try three minutes of quiet three times per day for ten days. Ask your higher self during these times: "What advice do you have for me today?"

7_____ Are you getting at least seven hours of sleep per night?

8_____ Are you focusing on the beauty of your body? What is your favorite part?

9_____ Have you had a medical checkup?

10_____ Have you had a colonoscopy? (Applicable only if you are a candidate for this procedure, usually people over fifty years.)

11_____ Do you detoxify? Fresh squeezed lime juice in a glass of water each morning may help reduce acidity and increase alkalinity.

12_____ Do you exfoliate? Make way for the new.

13_____ Are you optimistic? Is your life getting better or worse?

14_____ Are you satisfied with your life? Do you complain that you have too much; too busy, too much stress, too many people depending on you? Consider the phrase: "It is what I think it is." These "too much" situations can be turned into gratitude that your life is so full.

15_____ Do you have a positive attitude? How are you? "Medium." "I'm tired." "I'm old." Does this sound like you? Can you turn it around and focus on what is going well?

16_____ Do you have friends with a positive attitude?

17_____ Do you love?

18_____ Do you laugh?

19_____ Do you have "emotional vitality: a sense of enthusiasm, hopefulness, engagement?" In her 2007 Harvard study, Laura Kubzansky, associate professor of social and behavioral sciences and director of the Society and Health Psychophysiology Laboratory at the Harvard School of Public Health, found that emotional vitality—a sense of enthusiasm, of hopefulness, of engagement in life, and the ability to face life's stresses with emotional balance—appears to reduce the risk of coronary heart disease.

20_____ Do you share twenty hugs per day? I like giving hugs and getting hugs, but sharing hugs is my favorite. Can you feel the difference in your attitude when you share a hug?

Out of a potential 200 points, how did you rate yourself? Are you satisfied with the results? Are your low rated answers within your circle of influence so that you can change them? Choose the statements on which you scored the lowest. Think about ways you can improve your score and take action.

The connection of the mind/body is being studied and researched at institutions and universities around the world. There is no denying that it exists and it has an impact on our lives every minute of the day.

How much scientific research do you need to prove that when you are happy and ZESTY you feel better?

I have a friend, Elaine Lindsay, who suffers from many physical ailments due to a horrendous automobile accident that happened many years ago and the complications of the ensuing botched surgery. She lost a large piece of her leg. She doesn't take a single step without being conscious of how she is going to do it. What has gotten her through - and I am certain that research would validate it - is that her positive attitude and sense of humor help her. Her smiling face and her courage lifts my spirits every time I see her.

> **Affirmation:**
> **I dedicate myself to improving**
> **my mind/body checklist score.**

Chapter 11
Mind/Mental Aspect

*"The essence of a person arises from the existence of
mental functions which permit him or her to think
and to perceive, to love and to hate, to learn and to
remember, to solve problems, to communicate through
speech and writing, to create and to destroy civilizations.*

*These expressions are closely related with brain
functioning. Therefore, without the brain, the mind
cannot exist, without the behavioral manifestation, the
mind cannot be expressed."*

—Dr. Silvia Helena Cardoso

The brain is the organ that controls and operates your body. It is a part of your central nervous system along with your spinal cord. To serve you well, it needs to be healthy. The brain is 75 percent water and needs to be constantly replenished. Dehydration can cause fatigue, confusion, headaches, stress, and lack of mental focus. If your body is not healthy and strong, your mind suffers, and your ZEST is greatly depleted.

The mind and the body are in constant communication. The mind can have a positive or negative influence on your body and vice versa. You can see this positive influence with young children when they get excited and they can't stop themselves from jumping. You can see that the happiness is overwhelming. You can see the negative influence on the body in people who have suffered from post-traumatic stress and become ill. In both of these examples, the mind overtakes the body and creates a physical response.

Do you believe you are worthy and deserve to be a ZEST-filled woman? If this is what you want then don't sabotage yourself; change your beliefs to know that you deserve to have your dreams come true. Be kind to yourself.

The mind/mental aspect could easily be called the *air aspect* or *wind aspect*. The mind is strong, changing, and moving like the wind. It is closely linked to the emotional aspect. The mind is the mental aspect where you anchor your beliefs, create expectations, set boundaries, and make commitments.

As the global population of baby boomers age, more attention than ever is being focused on keeping the mind active by participating in learning new things such as dancing, music, or a new language. I find it interesting that the philosophy that is applied to helping the aging population is the same philosophy that is utilized to help children develop to their fullest potential.

A.A. Milne's *Winnie the Pooh* is busy learning new things, solving mysteries, and asking Owl many questions. "Think, think, think, that's all I do," said Winnie the Pooh.

States of Conscious and Levels of Awareness

The definitions of states of consciousness and levels of awareness range from narrow to broad. The science and research behind them are complicated; the messages are not. I will share my understanding and application.

Unconsciousness refers to having no awareness of yourself and/or your environment. Consider the child jumping up and down with excitement;

she is not even aware that she is doing it. Unconsciousness is also having no awareness of the impact of your behavior on others, like talking too loudly on a cell phone in a public place. While texting on your phone you may become so engrossed that you are unaware of your environment.

Most of the time, we are not conscious of the body processes controlled by our mind. When we are healthy, we breathe unconsciously, but now that I mentioned it you've become conscious of your breathing. Where your breathing is concerned, you have shifted your level of awareness from unconscious breathing to conscious breathing. You are conscious of your breathing and you are conscious that you are reading this book. You are focused and aware.

Consciousness is the state of awareness of your environment and yourself. When you are learning a new skill, you give it your full attention and focus; you are conscious of your every move. You gain proficiency by repeating the skill, and then you can do it with less conscious focus. Learning how to drive is a good example. You can drive, talk to someone, and do probably too many other things at the same time. However, is different than developing a *conscience*, which is discerning right from wrong.

Subconscious awareness occurs when you are not consciously aware of something, but your behavior shows that it exists. Many years ago, when my daughter was a young teenager, I had the opportunity to show her what subconscious behavior was like. It was my colleague's birthday and I hosted a small birthday celebration for him in our office. Moments before his girlfriend came in, I told my daughter to observe the girlfriend's behavior. After greeting everyone, she stood behind his chair and put her hand on his shoulder, petted him, and was obviously and subconsciously marking her territory. It's a lesson my daughter never forgot.

The subconscious mind holds the memories and beliefs of all our experiences. If you hold negative beliefs about yourself, then finding the root cause of the problem may be possible by exploring your subconscious. Subconscious memories and beliefs may sabotage conscious intentions. You may need to reprogram your subconscious to take control of your life. Access to these memories varies. We may be able to recall them and process them ourselves, or we may need the guidance of a trained professional.

Levels of consciousness are like a light with a dimmer switch. The more awareness you have of your consciousness and feelings, the more you are able to consciously choose your response.

Superconsciousness is living in full awareness of the world around you, as well as your feelings and environment. You are also attuned to the changing moods, feelings, and sensitivities of those around you. You recognize when you're feeling charged or emotional; you can trace those times to the experiences that created the beliefs at the source of your feelings. Most importantly, your superconsciousness facilitates *changing your feelings* at will.

A superconsciousness level of awareness is also present when you are totally engrossed and focused on what you are doing, while at the same time monitoring the environment, your feelings, and the feelings of others. You are *in the flow* of what you are doing, creating, and experiencing.

Your superconscious mind is controlled by your thought patterns, which are anchored in your beliefs and create your physical reality. Listen to the voices in your mind that are positive, reassuring, and encouraging; they support your dreams and desires. Your inner dialogue gives you the strength, power, courage, and confidence to grow, expand, and be where you are today, and take you where you want to go tomorrow.

Fear

Humans are predisposed to avoid change and fear the unknown. This state of being is what kept our ancestors safe. Our ancestors were fearful enough not to step into a dark cave without knowing if it did or didn't have a dangerous animal in it.

A mindset of fear, helplessness, and victimization stops you in your tracks instantly. These are the mental barriers that hold you back from your dreams and desires. An inner dialogue that depletes you and leaves you feeling helpless and victimized never serves you. Being abusive and demeaning to yourself and/or others sabotages you; the negative energy blocks your intent to manifest positive energy and abundance of your dreams and desires.

Is the nonstop thinking box that you carry on your shoulders a burden of worry, doubt, and fear? Are you wallowing in past mistakes and fear of the future? This campaign is being led by the "itty-bitty-shitty committee" and it is trying to keep your ZEST from coming through. It is easily recognizable by the monologue of limiting beliefs. "I'm not good enough." "I'm not ready." "Who do I think I am to do this?" "I can't do this." "What will people think?"

These liars don't have your best interests in mind. It's time the itty-bitty-shitty committee got FIRED!

Mental Health

Finally, after years of being swept aside, mental health is being discussed in the media. From the Canadian Mental Health Association website: www.cmha.ca

Who is affected by mental illness?

- Mental illness indirectly affects all Canadians at some time through a family member, friend, or colleague.

- 20 percent of Canadians will personally experience a mental illness in their lifetime.

- Mental illness affects people of all ages, educational and income levels, and cultures.

- Approximately 8 percent of adults will experience major depression at some time in their lives.

- What causes it? (These are the top two causes listed.)

- A complex interplay of genetic, biological, personality, and environmental factors causes mental illnesses.

- Almost one half (49 percent) of those who feel they have suffered from depression or anxiety have never gone to see a doctor about this problem.

Dealing with and managing mental health issues with yourself and those around you can be a large barrier. Please seek professional help or support if you fall into this category.

Be gentle with yourself and apply the exercises necessary to shift your mindset and open your heart.

"Hurdles are made to jump over."
—Nick Cannon

Chapter 12
The Body

"If you don't take care of your body, where are you going to live?"
—Unknown

Your body is the physical aspect that hosts your emotional, mental, spiritual, and sensual core aspects. As previously discussed, research has proven that a healthy body leads to a positive mindset and happier life.

Too often, women ignore their bodies and push themselves into a state of exhaustion. Being tired is okay, but we must learn not to exhaust our reserves. It dishonors Grandmother Earth.

Bone Density

In 1997, Dr. Miriam E. Nelson published her book, *Strong Women Stay Young,* based on her study to examine how strength training might affect bone density and risk factors for osteoporosis for women in midlife and older. Her study followed forty postmenopausal women for a year. All were healthy, but sedentary and none were taking hormones. Half the volunteers, the control group, simply maintained their usual lifestyle. The others went to the Tufts University laboratories twice a week and lifted weights.

Most women begin to lose bone and muscle mass at about age forty; in part because of this, they *choose* to start to slow down. That's exactly what happened to the women who didn't exercise. One sedentary year later, their muscles and bones had aged and they were even less active than before.

The women who lifted weights changed too, but in the opposite direction. After one year of strength training, their bodies were fifteen to twenty years more youthful. They became stronger, often even stronger than when they were younger. Without drugs, they regained bone density, which helped to prevent osteoporosis. Their balance and flexibility improved. They were leaner and trimmer, though eating as much as ever. The women were so energized, they became 27 percent more active. Learn more about this program at www.StrongWomen.com.

Your body dictates what it wants and it shows you where to focus, as long as you're paying attention! When you feel overall body aches and pains in muscles and/or joints, that's your body changing patterns—getting you unstuck or telling you to get up and get moving.

Exercise, including walking and weight lifting, releases oxytocin, which makes you feel happier, healthier, and more ZESTY. Your body is influencing your mind; your experience of being physically active changes your belief in yourself and your ability. There are great stories about people being able to overcome physical impairments through their deliberate intent to heal themselves and take action. To change your body, it is mandatory that you take *action.*

See your health professional before starting any new physical regime. If you need help, enroll in a program, ask a friend or neighbor for suggestions, or hire a personal trainer to customize your program.

CHAKRAS

Chakra is the Sanskrit word meaning wheel or vortex. Chakras are spiral pools of rotating, vibrating energy in our bodies. Although not part of the physical body, they have powerful influence on vitality, well-being, and life force. I'm introducing them here because they offer one more way to understand the energy of the mind/body connection.

The chakras' energy goes through the entire body. They are each associated with a color, element, and presence—and they rotate at increasing speeds; the first chakra being the slowest and the seventh being the fastest. It's fun to imagine the chakra's location, color, which is the same as a rainbow, and element, and to explore how it feels to associate with it.

Note the Seven Major Chakras

Chakra	Location	Color	Element	Associated with
1—root	tailbone	red	earth	physical presence
2—sacral	two fingers below the navel	orange	water	sexuality, emotions
3—solar plexus	upper abdomen	yellow	fire	power, vitality
4—heart	heart	green	air	love
5—throat	throat	blue	sound	communication
6—third eye	brow	indigo	intuition	intuition
7—crown	top of head	violet	understanding	understanding

When I meditate on the chakras, I always start at the tailbone/derrière and work my way up, breathing the energy in and exhaling any negative associations. Create your own meditation and understanding of the chakras or use mine:

- *First chakra:* I picture a red spiral of energy coming from the earth, anchoring and grounding me in my body. I feel safe, secure, and at peace. Breathe the energy in and exhale any negative associations.

- *Second chakra:* I put my hand on my tummy as I see a lovely orange globe that fills the space with water. My emotions flow freely and I feel the pleasure, power, and creativity of my passion and intimacy. Breathe the energy in and exhale anything associated with guilt, fear, and blame. Let them flow away. Accept that they happened and forgive yourself. Hidden in the same area is the womb chakra, which is the center of all creation and seat of the soul. When the womb chakra is healed, relationships flourish, painful past relationships are dissolved, and a powerful connection is created with the divine.

- *Third chakra:* I put my hand slightly above my waist and I see the bright yellow fire that fuels me. I feel alive, vital, and confident. I have my personal willpower to take action to fulfill my dreams and desires. I breathe the energy in and unblock any shame and negative associations when I exhale. I forgive myself.

- *Fourth chakra:* I put my hand on my heart and I feel love and warmth. I am compassionate, kind, and loving. I see the beauty of the color green after a long, white winter. I breathe in the energy of love and exhale all my grief, sadness, and loss out in front of me. I let the pain flow out of my body and essence.

- *Fifth chakra:* I put my hand gently on my throat and I imagine a beautiful, blue, spiraling sphere guiding my communication. I speak openly and honesty. My words to myself and others are kind, truthful, and supportive. Breathe in the calm energy and exhale any negative associations.

- *Sixth chakra:* I massage the space between my eyes and a bit above my eyebrows, as I listen for insights and intuition to be downloaded. Breathe the energy in of being connected to everyone and everything. Exhale any illusions that are blocking the flow and growth. Indigo light may appear. To open your mind's eye and reach a higher state of consciousness, saying "AUM" may be soothing and helpful.

Joseph Campbell has the following conversation with Bill Moyers in *The Power of Myth:*

CAMPBELL: "AUM" is a word that represents to our ears that sound of the energy of the universe of which all things are manifestations. You start in the back of the mouth "ahh," and then "oo," you fill the mouth, and "mm" closes the mouth. When you pronounce this properly, all vowel sounds are included in the pronunciation. AUM. Consonants are here regarded simply as interruptions of the essential vowel sound. All words are thus fragments of AUM, just as all images are fragments of the Form of forms. AUM is a symbolic sound that puts you in touch with that resounding being that is the universe. If you heard some of the recordings of Tibetan monks chanting AUM, you would know what the word means. That's the AUM of being in the world. To be in touch with that and to get the sense of that is the peak experience of all.

A-U-M. The birth, the coming into being, and the dissolution that cycles back. AUM is called the "four-element syllable." A-U-M and what is the fourth element? The silence out of which AUM arises, back into which it goes, and what underlies it. My life is the A-U-M, but there is a silence underlying it, too. That is what we would call the immortal. This is the mortal and that's the immortal and there wouldn't be the mortal if there weren't the immortal. One must discriminate between the mortal aspect and the immortal aspect of one's own existence. In the experience of my mother and father, who are gone and of whom I was born, I have come to understand that there is more than what was our temporal relationship. Of course there were certain moments in that relationship when an emphatic demonstration of what the relationship was would be brought to my realization. I clearly remember some of those. They stand out as moments of epiphany, of revelation, of the radiance.

MOYERS: The meaning is essentially wordless.

CAMPBELL: Yes. Words are always qualifications and limitations.

MOYERS: And yet, Joe, all we puny human beings are left with is this miserable language, beautiful though it is, that falls short of trying to describe—

CAMPBELL: That's right, and that's why it is a peak experience to break past all that, every now and then, and to realize, "Oh . . . ah. . . ."

- *Seventh chakra:* I picture a beautiful violet lotus flower, spiraling a greater level of awareness and understanding of the cosmic energy for myself and others. I feel joy and bliss in my connection to the universe. I breathe the energy in and surrender myself to let go of any negative associations when I exhale. Chakra meditation aligns the entire body's energy and calms the mind. When the mind is calm it listens more acutely and has sharp, clear thoughts and reasoning abilities. Keeping the body in strong, healthy condition is ideal. There is a popular belief that your body is designed to balance and heal itself. That may have some validity, but I think we should do everything that we can to work with the body and do as little as we can to harm it.

UNIVERSAL LIFE FORCE ENERGY

There is a universal life force energy and without it we have no life. The entire world is fueled by it. It endures all time, space, and dimensional realities. Every living thing in the world starts and is sustained by life force energy.

Life force energy is the spark that moves us to take action to transform our dreams, desires, and wishes into reality. It is the drive, passion, and determination that puts you into action to take on a challenging dream, job, or project.

It pulls the emotional, mental, physical, and spiritual energies together. It creates the catalyst energy that increases the amount and intensity of ZEST that you access and utilize to take action. Imagination is sparked and action is fueled by life force energy. It is the energy surge that you feel when you tell your power-filled ZEST stories.

Life force energy may also be experienced in the physical act of love making. It may motivate you and drive you to have hot, passionate sex. It is the life force energy that you feel when you have an orgasm. There are some exceptions, but I like to think that most of us are here because at least one person had something: an orgasm. We would not be here today without it.

When life force energy is absent, your dreams and desires are stuck in fantasy, illusion, and wishful thinking. Your thinking becomes stagnant and your life becomes pedestrian.

It is the catalyst and essence necessary to *ZEST Your Life* and when we open our hearts and mind to bond with it, our entire life changes. It puts ZEST on turbo power.

CHAPTER 13
BARRIERS TO BODY ZEST

It is a fact of nature that the body does go through changes, which can be challenging for us. It is also a fact that our society, for the most part, has developed in a manner that is not conducive to treating our bodies with love, care, and respect. Many people have fallen into the stressed lifestyle that starts with a coffee and a donut, which I can't even dignify by calling breakfast. On a weekly basis the news reports the statistics of increased heart disease, cancer, diabetes, etc. We can put the odds on our side by removing the barriers that hold us back from having a healthier body.

HEART DISEASE

Until recently, heart disease was the number one killer of women. A Swedish study examined thirty-two pairs of identical twins. One twin in each pair had heart disease, and the other was healthy. The researchers found that weight, smoking status, and cholesterol levels of each of the twins really weren't very different. But one of the significant differences was "poor childhood and adult interpersonal relationships"; being able to resolve conflicts and how much emotional support they got from other people made the difference (excerpt from *Looking Out/Looking In*). This study supports the idea that your mind can and does influence your body.

THYROID

Are you tired? The thyroid gland helps regulate energy. Are your eyebrows getting thinner and shorter on the outside? This can be a symptom of thyroid malfunction. Check your thyroid by getting a blood test and discuss the result with your health practitioner.

CANCER

How many people think that cancer is hereditary? Fact: Only 10 percent of cancers are genetic. If you believe that you will have cancer at age forty because your mother and your grandmother had cancer at age forty, what do you think that belief does to your odds?

"A meticulous 1987 study from Yale, reported by M.R. Jensen, found that breast cancer spread fastest among women who had repressed personalities, felt hopeless, and were unable to express anger, fear, and other negative emotions. Similar findings have emerged for rheumatoid arthritis, asthma, intractable pain, and other disorders."

IMMUNE SYSTEM

Besides being unhealthy on their own, each of these may deplete your immune system and cause other physical symptoms of being tired, weight loss or gain, trouble sleeping, etc.

- Infection

- Depression

- Always being on the defensive and armoring yourself from the world

- Anger and fear, which are an exhausting waste of energy and make you tired

> **Affirmation:**
> **I am complaint free and happier.**

AGING

> *"Age is an issue of mind over matter. If you don't*
> *mind, it doesn't matter."*
> —*Mark Twain*

All of these barriers also make you old. Some people are old at fifty and others are vital, fit, and ZESTY at ninety-five or more. Human aging is fluid and even reversible, as Dr. Miriam Nelson discovered.

Aging biomarkers are those things that tell you how old you would be if you didn't know how old you were. In *Biomarkers,* Evans and Rosenberg isolated the following ten signposts of vitality that can be altered for the better by changes in lifestyle:

1. Muscle mass

2. Strength

3. Basal metabolic rate (calculated weight/height/age for caloric need)

4. Body fat percentage

5. Aerobic capacity

6. Blood-sugar tolerance

7. Cholesterol/HDL ratio

8. Blood pressure

9. Bone density

10. Ability to regulate internal temperature

All ten biomarkers can be revived or improved significantly through strength training.

BELIEFS AND TRAUMA

Modeling, programming, and experience form the beliefs, attitudes, and opinions that you have now. You have been molded and sculpted by your image makers.

Sexual assault, rape, and incest are not sex; they are acts of violence and certainly are barriers to ZEST. Unfortunately, the statistics for the number of women, and the increasing number of men, who are victims of these crimes are rising. Overcoming these traumas is not easy, but you are not alone; it is likely that most of the women around you have had their own negative experiences. Don't let the perpetrators hold onto your power. Heal these traumas and get your power back so that you can enjoy life.

Unwanted pregnancy also can be a barrier to permitting yourself to enjoy physical ZEST and the pure joy of the energy. You can change your thoughts and beliefs by focusing on and understanding the experiences that created them.

- What beliefs and rules do you have about your physical sensuality and sexuality? What rules were imposed on you? Do you feel like they're strangling you?

- Describe your sexual history and experiences and explore what they say about your life.

- Do you (or did you) consider sex to be all physical or do you link sex on an emotional and spiritual basis? In other words, do you need to have an emotional feeling for someone before you engage physically with him or her?

- Verbal programming: When you were a child what did you hear about sex?

- Modeling: When you were young what did you see?

- Specific incidents: What pleasant and unpleasant experiences did you have related to sexuality and sensuality when you were young? Did you have pleasant experiences? Or was sexual assault, rape, or incest your experience?

Your beliefs today are based on your past. Are these beliefs still valid or do you want to change your beliefs and base them on what you know to be true for you now?

You can also do this exercise with your partner. Discuss the history each of you brings to to the table about sex. Also, find out what sex really means to your partner. Is it pleasure, freedom, security, or status? This assists you in identifying each other's current blueprint and may help you discover areas you have in common and areas you don't.

MONEY

Some may feel that money is a barrier to body ZEST. You don't need a fancy gym membership to get your body moving. If you don't have weights, then do what Ed Allan, the fitness guru, suggested over forty years ago: use cans of soup.

"ZEST is the secret of all beauty.
There is no beauty that is attractive without ZEST."
—*Christian Dior*

Affirmation:
My ZEST energy is strong and vibrant.
I contribute to the greatest good of all.

CHAPTER 14
MIND/BODY WORKING TOGETHER

The evidence of the mind/body connection is growing. The "Positive Emotions Build Physical Health" research, published in *Psychological Science,* 2013, suggests "that positive emotions, positive social connections, and physical health influence one another in a self-sustaining upward spiral dynamic."

The researchers summarized several sources that concluded, "Experiencing frequent positive emotions, for instance, forecasts having fewer colds, reduced inflammation, and less cardiovascular disease. Complementing this prospective correlational evidence, a recent field experiment found that individuals randomly assigned to self-generate positive emotions reported experiencing fewer headaches and less chest pain, congestion, and weakness..."

"...Intriguingly, recent prospective evidence suggests that the causal arrow between positive emotions and physical health may run in the opposite direction as well: physical health also appears to promote positive emotions..."

"...We propose here that people's ability to translate their own positive emotions into positive social connections with others may hold one of the keys to solving this mystery..."

"...Most advice dispensed about how people might improve their physical health calls for increased physical activity, improved nutritional intake, and reductions in tobacco and alcohol use. Alongside this good advice, we now have evidence to recommend efforts to self-generate positive emotions as well. Recurrent momentary experiences of positive emotions appear to serve as nutrients for the human body, increasing feelings of social belonging and giving a needed boost to parasympathetic health, which in turn opens people up to more and more rewarding positive emotional and social experiences. Over time, this self-sustaining upward spiral of growth appears to improve physical health…"

Mind/Body Connection to Disease

The mind/body connection is so strong that diseases can be linked to mental causes. Listen to your body. Here are some common associations:

- Stiff body—rigid personality

- Cold—worry about the future

- Eyes—refusing to see

- Ears—refusing to hear

- Neck, throat, teeth—expressing yourself

- Lower back—anger

The mind/body connection is so strong that if you do not create and live your life the way you want and instead you make yourself small, then you will get sick.

Personal Appearance and Image

How you think, feel, and express yourself has an energetic effect on your physical body. Research shows that your thoughts can change the chemistry in your body.

Mae West, an actress from the 1920's, was asked why she put so much effort into looking good. Her answer, "I owe it to my public." Personal appearance is how you look. Image is how other people see you and it is how you see yourself. Make a positive impression on yourself first!

How you dress matters. How you dress should always make you feel good about yourself. When you catch a glimpse of yourself in a mirror or shop window, how do you feel about it? Does the voice in your head say, "You look fabulous," or does the image make you rush past?

What conscious and unconscious message do you receive? Is that the message you want to send to yourself and others? Does the way you dress reflect who you are? Is that the energy you want to put out into the world?

Maximize your personal and professional image by developing a sense of style, impact, and identity. Maybe you want to change your hair color or style, have your ideal weight, and wear a more ZESTY style of clothing. Perhaps you want to workout to have a healthier body, discover a new relationship, and develop a deeper interest in your career.

Ponder the reasons you want to make these changes. Delve deep within yourself to consider why making these changes is important to you. Were you bullied in school and don't feel positive about yourself? Do you believe you can move closer toward the type of life you want if you make the desired changes?

Perhaps you think you'll be happier or more successful when you take steps to become the person you want to be. Giving some thought to the reasons you want to change these aspects of yourself helps you recognize where you want to be in life. Design a brief plan for each area you want to alter.

What do you want to see in the mirror? Getting a different hair color or cut is as simple as setting an appointment and going to the hairdresser. Doing a wardrobe overhaul doesn't have to cost a lot of money or you can obtain the clothing you want little by little. Adding a ZESTY scarf or accessory allows you to try different styles. Consult fashion magazines and websites to learn about styles and basic wardrobe pieces.

Achieving an improved body and your ideal weight may take a bit more thought and effort. What are you doing to get started on your plan now? It always helps to reduce the unhealthy stress in your life. You might cut out or reduce soft drinks, alcohol, and fattening, sugary food. Start by having healthy breakfasts of oatmeal and fruit or a scrambled egg with toast.

You might experience doubt, hesitancy, or procrastination to avoid getting started. Connect with your feelings to be successful in creating a new you. Explore how you feel about working toward the changes. Stop, breathe, and listen to your inner knowing. Do one small thing, one small step in the direction you have targeted. If you have doubts or fears about taking steps toward what you want in life, consider contacting me for a personal one-on-one session to help you move forward in your quest.

Do you feel positive, confident, and pleased that you're finally going to "do something"? What makes you feel that way? This step is integral to your capacity to continue your path of transformation and self reinvention. Put your plans into action. If all systems are "go," move forward without delay. Notice the subtle changes that you achieve along the way. Develop ways to reinforce your efforts to successfully alter the aspects you wish to change. Take a few pictures of yourself as you notice changes and display them for motivation. After all, you're doing what you set out to do to ZEST your life!

Creating a new and improved *you* can be an exciting time in your life. Embrace this phase of life with everything you have. You're worth it.

"Dress for success, wear a smile!"
—*Unknown*

CHAPTER 15
BARRIERS TO MIND/BODY ZEST

Barriers are obstacles, stumbling blocks, or hurdles that we must be aware of and then we must shrink them, push them aside, or overcome them. The following barriers are crippling to many people; don't be one of those people. You may need to seek professional help to change the habits that might have become addictions. Nutritional counseling can provide you with healthy alternatives. If this is you, you are not alone. Take good care of yourself.

JUNK FOOD

What foods make your stomach churn and your body weak? On our way to a ski trip, my husband and I stopped for fish and chips, which is something we rarely do. By the time we got to the ski hill, we both felt tired, sleepy, and without any energy. We were so sluggish that we ended up going home.

Sluggish food = sluggish body = sluggish mind.

Junk food for the body affects the mind.

TOXIC THOUGHTS ARE JUNK FOOD FOR THE MIND

Good food = good body (having energy) = a happy mind. Digesting good thoughts is like digesting good food. Replace toxic beliefs, emotions, relationships, food, etc., with helpful and healthy beliefs, emotions, love, relationships, food, etc. In Chinese medicine, emotions and organs are directly linked, so it's not surprising that stress can give you a painful stomach.

What thoughts make your stomach churn? Trying to digest nastiness and bad thoughts is junk food for the mind. Toxic thoughts go to the cellular body and DNA holds ancestral memories of all experiences. Release and remove mind toxins before they pollute your body.

> *"You are a child of God. Your playing small does not serve the world. There is nothing enlightened about shrinking so that other people won't feel insecure around you. We are all meant to shine, as children do. We were born to make manifest the glory of God that is within us. It's not just in some of us; it's in everyone. And as we let our own light shine, we unconsciously give other people permission to do the same. As we are liberated from our own fear, our presence automatically liberates others."*
> —*Marianne Williamson*

COMPLAINING

Inspired by David R. Hamilton, PhD

Learn more at: www.AComplaintFreeWorld.org

Non-Complaining Challenge

The twenty-one day non-complaining challenge involves wearing an elastic band on your wrist, and every time you complain, even if it's solely thinking of a complaint, change the elastic from one wrist to the other. Encourage the people around you to join the fun. By the way, any sentence that starts with a curse or swear word is probably going to be a complaint.

In this exercise, you'll be surprised at how difficult it is not to complain, especially while driving. It eliminates complaints, judgments, criticisms, and heightens your awareness.

Often, thoughts are expressed as complaints. Rework your vocabulary to express your desires without complaining. For example, change: "I always get stuck doing this" to "I would really appreciate it if you would help me with this." Show your gratitude by offering to do something with others in return.

> *"A house is no home unless it contains food and fire for the mind as well as the body."*
> —*Margaret Fuller*

The mind/mental aspect, or the wind aspect, can be changed from a hurricane wind that is wreaking havoc and destruction to a calm breeze of peace and serenity. Calm that wind by applying ZESTERS to your everyday life.

Mind/body ZEST at high measure uplifts you and the people around you into a positive energy of beauty and vibrant life. It is a simple idea to think that being happy feels good. It releases endorphins in the brain. If you're not feeling happy, put a smile on your face and act like you are; soon you'll start to feel better. Even if you don't start out happy, when your brain releases these endorphins you become happy. You may not be skipping down the street like you're in a Viagra commercial, but you'll feel better.

CHAPTER 16
PART 3 ZESTERS

These ZESTERS bring fast, proven results. They each release endorphins and oxytocin to the brain to make you feel good in all aspects (physical, emotional, mental and spiritual).

- Speak to yourself and others with kindness. Help others find comfort and happiness.

- Forgive yourself for the times when you let go of your ZEST and your beautiful, positive thoughts.

- Let go of the fear, and find love. That's where the ZEST is.

- In times of conflict or fear, open your heart, and flood the space with love. Practice doing that now. You are safe. Stand up, open your hands and your heart, open your arms, and flood the space with love; pull it all in, and put your hands on your heart. Can you feel the difference in you and in the space around you? HEART HEART HEART

"Turns out, you should never say never. In fact, doing the thing you say you would never do has the potential to crack your heart and mind wide open to possibilities you never thought were available to YOU."
—*Susana Frioni*

- Dream the best dreams possible for yourself. Having dreams and hope for the future is important to your mental health and the health of those around you. When you lose your dreams, you can't be there for the dreams of others.

- Dream pleasant dreams. Before you go to sleep, ask for pleasant dreams, and wish pleasant dreams to others. Pay attention and be aware of how lovely your wish for pleasant dreams makes you and others around you feel.

- With visualization, mind (brain) changes matter almost immediately. Visualization offers direction and purpose to dissolve old thoughts with new thoughts. Visualize a tiny image of yourself, possibly in full fighting armor with a sword and shield, for healing your mind, changing your beliefs, and shrinking the pain. Address the cause of the pain, as opposed to the pain itself. If thinking about something causes pain and hurts, it needs healing.

- Decide that you are going to have a good day. Don't fall for the crap that if you stub your toe getting out of bed it means you're going to have a bad day! Happy people decide they're going to be happy and they're going to have a good day. Choose to be content and happy.

- Drink plenty of water for brain and body health. Water cleanses the body and flushes out toxins. Have some now.

- Take a walk to clear your mind. While you are walking, be aware of your surroundings and how your body feels. Breathe deeply. Appreciate the trees and the nature that is all around you. Smile while you walk; the trees might smile back at you!

- Encode positive experiences in your body by being aware of your posture and your body. Pursue spinal alignment. Stand up and gently turn your palms out. This puts your shoulders and spine into alignment.

> **Affirmation:**
> **I am proud to stand tall in my power and ZEST.**

- Your body is stronger when you think positive thoughts. Lift weights or pump your arms up and down a few times while thinking sad thoughts; as you pump, change your sad thoughts to happy thoughts. The happier your thoughts, the stronger you feel! Feel the difference in how much more weight you can lift or how much less effort it takes when you're happy.

- Lift weights. A mere twenty minutes, three times a week and you can see and feel the difference in as little as two or three weeks.

> **Affirmation:**
> **Happy thoughts make my body strong.**

- Include physical play in your life. Dancing is easy physical play. "Dance like no one is watching." If you can't dance, then sway to the music.

- Watch your body posture. How does your body feel? It's hard to have pride in yourself if you walk around slouched and look and feel full of shame and regret. Sitting up straight tells your mind to pay attention. Take an example from Olympic figure skaters; they always have perfect posture.

- Spend time with happy people. To learn how to be happy; find happy people and spend time with them. Watch what they do. Do they criticize? Do they complain? No, not much.

- Love. You can fall in love every day. Fall in love with your life and love yourself.

- Draw strong, masculine energy from the sun to give you strength to take action. Make a triangle with your thumbs touching and your index fingers touching. Hold your arms up and look at the sun in the triangle. Then bring the triangle into your womb space with the apex pointing down.

- Utilize the moon. Pay attention to the moon and its effects on your body. The moon is the feminine; it regulates menstrual cycles and can be a source of power and energy. Are you seeding new intentions during the new moon? Give gratitude for the fullness of your life at full moon.

- Draw from the full moon. Make a triangle with your thumbs touching and your index fingers touching. Hold your arms up, and look at the full moon in the triangle. Then bring the triangle into your womb space with the apex pointing down. Ask the moon for the strength and power to help you.

- Draw from the rain. Ask for emotions to be cleansed and negativity to be washed away—down to your feet—and transformed to nourish Mother Earth.

- Draw from the stars or your favorite constellation. Ask the Seven Sisters of the Pleiades (M 45 on astronomy charts and maps) to guide you, as they have guided explorers on the seas and people all over the world.

- Enjoy what is around you at this very moment. Enjoy the rain, the snow, the sun, the dark, the stars, and the moon.

- Use aromatherapy. Aromatherapy is the use of plant extracts that have particular healing properties. The essential oils can be used in massages, baths, closets, drawers—anywhere you want to benefit from breathing in the healing energy. I keep lavender aromatherapy oil in my linen closet. Every time I open the door, I get the divine, soothing, and relaxing scent.

- Engage flower essences. Bach's® Flower Remedy, in particular Rescue Remedy, was designed for veterans returning from the war and suffering from shell shock. The original Bach Flower Remedies is a system of thirty-eight flower remedies that correct emotional imbalances; negative emotions are replaced with positive. For more information go to www.BachFlower.com.

- Create and utilize your sacred space. Establish a special place where you can be have peace and quiet. It could be a special room, an office, the bathroom, the shower, or even the closet.

- Balance your home. Does your physical living space feel in balance? Where does your body live? Does your living space reflect who you are? Do vibrations of love, peace, and harmony surround you? Is it a sanctuary for everyone who enters? What can you do to spruce it up and increase the positive energy vibration? Keep the higher vibration by cleaning out closets and cupboards. Enjoy some flowers; even plastic flowers are cheerful and bright!

- Start a weekly giveaway campaign. My daughter and her husband both had completely furnished homes when they were single; then they received lots of wedding gifts. Today, they want to finish the basement, but they have so much "stuff." Recently, they gave away their dog crate and then a complete set of dishes, cutlery, a blender, and even the cappuccino maker. This was sure to spruce up their vibration and make room for new energy.

- Do the "Hestia Thing." One morning, my husband started cleaning off the top of his dresser—unusual behavior indeed. I asked him what was on his mind. He said, "Nothing, why do you ask?" I told him he was doing the "Hestia Thing ." Hestia is the Greek Goddess of the Hearth. When my husband was done cleaning the dresser he had found the answer to a problem that he had not been able to resolve at the office. If you find yourself head first in a closet, a drawer, or a pile of junk and you are making order out of chaos take note of how you feel after you're done. Have you resolved a dilemma or problem? You may emerge with a clean closet and an uncluttered mind. The Hestia Thing came to me too. My garden and internal self are mirror reflections of each other. One winter, the man who snow blows my driveway blew stones into my garden; it was a mess and so was my life. In the spring, I was in the garden and asked the Spirit, "What should I do to clean this up?" The answer came back loud and clear: "One at a time, Linda, one at a time." I needed to clean up my garden and my life, one small stone—one small step—at a time. I call it doing the Hestia Thing. As the lifestyle guru Martha Stewart says, "It's a good thing".

- Use mind/body stones. You stand and live on a mineral planet. The healing properties of the mineral world are well known. There are crystals in computers and watches. You can collect stones any-where; remember to say thank you to the earth for providing them. Keep them in your pocket or on your dresser, desk, or window sill. Cleanse or recharge the energy with running water or the light of the full moon.

ZEST Stones

My friend, Charles Brand, has pulled together a list of stones that are best for ZEST: ametrine (natural), *labradorite, opal, rhodochrosite, ruby, *selenite, Tibetan black quartz, *tiger eye.

The asterisk (*) indicates that these minerals are best suited for emo-tional ZEST.

- Breathe. Your breath is the air that gives you life from your first breath and keeps you alive to your last. Adults breathe twelve to twenty times per minute; that's about twenty-three thousand times a day.

Here's how it works. You breathe in through your nose and/or mouth, the air is filtered through the lungs, oxygen travels through a series of lung membranes into the blood, and the oxygenated blood courses through your entire body. On exhalation, impurities such as carbon dioxide are moved out of the body through the mouth and nose. Your body's blood is cleansed this way each day. In with the good and out with the bad.

Deep breathing is especially good for you because it utilizes the entire lung to bring in more oxygen and to expel more impurities. Deep breathing and making full use of your lungs provides maximum oxygen to the blood, the body, and the brain. If you have ever been unable to breathe, been stuffed up, or had a cold for a few days, you can appreciate what a magnificent body system we have.

In moments of shock, you may gasp and take a breath in and hold your breath for a moment. In moments of anxiety, you likely breathe shallow, short breaths at the top of your lungs. These are the times when you especially need take oxygen in and expel the impurities. So breathe deeply.

Athletes, musicians, and singers all train their breathing techniques for maximum efficiency—not only to oxygenate, but also to quiet and focus their minds. Have you ever tried to draw or paint a straight line? Your line is straighter when you paint or draw it on the exhalation of your breath. When you lift weights, breathing out during the lift gives you more strength.

BREATHE

Stand up, arms to the side with your hands open and facing front. Breathe into the full capacity of your lungs; your chest and stomach should expand and when you breathe out they flatten.

> *"Breathe in: 'I see my heart'.*
> *Breathe out: 'I smile at my heart'."*
> —*Yvonne Jennings, Swan Hill, Australia, ZEST Your Life*
> *program participant*

After a few breaths, you feel energized and cleansed.

Affirmation:
I breathe in love, I breathe in life.

- Enjoy pleasure. Our bodies are organic, pleasure seeking organisms. Feeling pleasure in your body clears your mind, improves your health, and increases your self-confidence. Like the song *Sweet Inspiration* says, "There ain't no telling what a satisfied woman might do." Life is a journey, always moving forward with no reverse; consciously take one step at a time in the right direction.

CALL TO ACTION

Part 3 contains a long list of ZESTERS to connect the mind/body; pick a few that you can implement today!

Complete this sentence: "I ZEST my mind/body by taking action and doing the following:

1.

2.

3.

To improve your body, you need the dedication and strength of a strong mind, and to have a powerful mind, you need a healthy body. If you struggle with the mind, work on the body for a while. If you struggle with the body, then exercise your mind with a new stimulating activity.

"Happiness is the consequence of personal effort... all sorrow
and trouble of this world is caused by unhappy people."
—*Elizabeth Gilbert*

Affirmation:

I am reaping the rewards of my personal effort.

Every little, positive action helps you feel better. When you feel better, you also feel more ZEST. So where does the ZEST come from? It comes from your private inner world. You can start by living your life in awareness, if you are not already doing so. If you already are, then expand it to every moment of every day, even when you are asleep. In your power-filled ZEST stories you have to find your authentic self and the power within and then build on that.

PART 4

LIVE YOUR ZEST!

"When sleeping women wake, mountains move."
—*Chinese Proverb*

It's time to move mountains. You have awakened the woman within. You have emotional maturity and your mind/body are connected. It's time to intend and manifest that this year and beyond do become the best years of your life.

Women hear and answer the call of inner knowing that power-filled ZEST moments do lead to a power-filled ZEST life, lining up like pearls on a string. The ZEST life calls on the ancient wisdom that is encoded in the feminine spirit. Being one with the rhythms of Mother Earth moves you from being self-centered or self-focused to knowing yourself well enough to contribute positively to the greater good. This can only be achieved if you live a power-filled ZEST life every day.

It is now time to balance the female and male powers. Modern societies have developed out of patriarchal cultures. This forms the understanding of power from a masculine, patriarchal point of view. This has placed half of the world population in a subservient and often victimized situation. We must now have a world that is from a balanced place of power. This does not make women the rulers of the future, but rather equal partners in making the world a better place for generations to come.

We are all connected to each other and what one person thinks or does affects the collective. There is a soul connection to each other, as the children of the earth. We are all the Universal Life Force Energy.

CHAPTER 17
WHAT IS SPIRITUAL ZEST?

"The Heart is where the Spirit is stored.
What I am calling Spirit is the energy that some others call Love...
This is what happens when we have a vision or a spiritual encounter...
We literally connect with the part of us that is a Universal Self,
the part of us that never disconnected from The All.
It is the part of us that is who we really are."
—Barbara Marx Hubbard

Spiritual ZEST is the influence, connection, and communication that you have with your higher self. To reinforce what Barbara Marx Hubbard says, "This is what happens when we open a channel for continuing dialogue with our Highest Self." Spiritual ZEST is manifested in activities that heal, renew, comfort, inspire, and lift you up.

A seventy-five year old woman recently shared with me the transcendent experience she had as a child receiving the sacrament of first communion in the Roman Catholic Church. As she described the feeling of light pouring over her and being directly connected to God, her face softened and she took me to that place with her. Starting from that moment she knew that she could talk to God and be heard.

Today, her double motto/mantra is "let go." "Ask." She puts her prayers in God's hands and lets go. Not long ago, she desperately wanted to go visit her sister who lived six hours away. She "asked", let go and stopped worrying about how it would happen, and opened herself to receive. Within five minutes her adult son came in the door, told her he was going to that city, and offered to drive her there and back. She experiences her first connection to spiritual ZEST again any time that she feels the need. You can do that too.

Feel Spiritual ZEST

Spirituality gives us hope and allows for the possibility that when we open our hearts, we can manifest our desires, our dreams will come true, and the unexplainable will happen. Expect the magic to happen, and it does.

One of the easiest ways to get to your core spiritual ZEST comes from reflecting on times when you were in that space and experiencing that feeling. Close your eyes and remember a time when you had what you would describe as a spiritual event, moment, or experience. It may have been when you participated in an activity that renewed, lifted, comforted, healed, and inspired you.

Take regular and easy flowing breaths. Your mind is quiet, your emotions are calm, your heart is expanded, and you feel an emotional, mental, and physical connection to the world. You have the connection to pure love in your heart. Go there now, and rediscover your inner light: the light that has always been there. The intent of this exercise is to remember a time when you felt spiritual ZEST at high measure and to hold onto that sacred feeling.

Affirmation:
I hold sacred the feeling of being in my spiritual ZEST.

*"A quiet awakening is under way across America as women
are coming together to worship, to tell their stories and to find
their place spiritually…God as a jealous, punitive white Anglo-
Saxon male with a long beard and a longer arm lacks appeal
for many contemporary women. This has led some to run into
the arms of the Goddess and find meaning in earth-centered
or neopagan rituals. It has led others to join Buddhist sanghas
where there is no personified God.*

*And it has led many more to question the relevance of their
religious beliefs to the homely realities of everyday life."*

—*Joan Borysenko*

My quest to make a connection to my higher self led me to study the Goddess and rediscover the feminine wisdom and power found in ancient myths and teachings. I realized that the stories connected with the characteristics of these archetypes could help me to recognize the gifts, strengths, and qualities that I hold.

Today, I am particularly fond of the following Goddesses because they help me to discern the qualities and characteristics that I want to emulate to deepen my spiritual ZEST:

- Celtic: Bridget—healing powers and survival are celebrated on February 1, the festival of Imbloc.

- Chinese: Kuan Yin shows compassion and mercy to all who suffer.

- Christian: Mary, the divine mother of Jesus Christ, is revered for taking care of her followers.

- Hawaiian: Pele appears as a woman just before a volcanic eruption. Gifts of food and tobacco to Pele are said to have resulted in the lava streams stopping before they reach the threatened village.

- Mayan: On Cozumel Island on the east coast of Mexico are the ruins of a shrine dedicated to Ix Chel. It was customary for women who wanted to become pregnant or wanted ease in childbirth to visit this shrine. San Gervasio Mayan Site ruins are open to the public.

- Greek: From *Goddesses in Every Woman* by Jean Shinoda Bolen, MD

Artemis, goddess of the hunt and the moon, personifies the independent, achievement oriented feminine spirit.

Athena, goddess of wisdom and craft, represents the logical, self-assured woman who is ruled by her head rather than her heart.

Hestia, goddess of the hearth, embodies the patient and steady woman who finds comfort in solitude and exudes a sense of intactness and wholeness.

Hera, goddess of marriage, stands for the woman who considers her roles as student, professional, or mother secondary to her essential goal of finding a husband and being married.

Demeter, goddess of grain and the maternal archetype, represents a woman's drive to provide physical and spiritual sustenance for her children.

Persephone, maiden and queen of the underworld, expresses a woman's tendency toward compliance, passivity, and a need to please and be wanted by others.

Aphrodite, goddess of love and beauty—the "alchemical" goddess governing a woman's enjoyment of love, beauty, sexuality, and sensuality—impels women to fulfill both creative and pro-creative functions.

More spiritual ZEST in life would certainly benefit the woman who is afraid to speak in public. She applies breathing techniques to overcome and calm the fear in her body. She focuses her mind to the benefits and the positive impact of her words. She invokes the courageous, achievement oriented feminine spirit to speak with eloquence and grace. After she has performed in public, she is grateful and humble for her success.

Spiritual ZEST is your direct connection to the holy, the divine, and the mysterious in yourself. You can rediscover your gifts, strengths, and qualities in the feminine wisdom and power found in ancient myths and teachings.

CHAPTER 18
BARRIERS TO SPIRITUAL ZEST

What are the barriers to feeling your spiritual ZEST all the time, more often, or at least once a day? What barriers prevent the influence, connection, and communication that links you to your higher self?

A major barrier may be that you don't take time for yourself. You don't pay attention to yourself because other things come first. Spiritual poverty alienates us from a full life.

There are times in everyone's lives when other things/people come first. Focusing on other people for a time is good; it can feed the soul. But there may be a time when you realize you are sacrificing your own care and well-being in the process. You may need to make a shift. This can create its own barrier as you try to change this pattern and stop being at others' beck and call. There may be resistance when you come back to knowing and being yourself. Even positive change can cause friction, especially when it involves other people in your life.

Barriers to spiritual ZEST also could be related to old wounds, rules, and experiences that shape your beliefs and keep you in fear. The spiritual awakening experience can make you a bit giddy and open sensations of energy surges, warmth, and vulnerability.

What other barriers are there? Work, phone, friends, children, email, family distractions, interruptions, other responsibilities? Did your schedule or relationships prevent you from going to a place of worship of your choice?

Barriers to spiritual ZEST deplete your energy; they leave you strung out and uninspired. Breathe deeply and take some time to discover what is in the way of connecting to your higher self. You've already discovered your greatest emotional mask—the beliefs and the thoughts associated with it. See Chapter Seven *Your Greatest Mask*. The barriers to spiritual ZEST need to be dismantled in almost the same way.

Follow these steps to uncover your spiritual connection:

- What is the greatest barrier that is stopping you from connecting to your higher self? Can you state only the facts? Take five minutes. You know you're finished when you start repeating yourself.

- How does it feel now in this moment? What are you thinking that is causing these feelings?

- What is the belief? Where and how did you acquire it?

- With what I know about the situation, is this true? Ask yourself again: "Am I sure it's true?" You may do some research by asking others who were there—family members and witnesses. But trust yourself to discern the truth. "With what I know about the situation, is this true?" "Is it true now?"

- Have your thoughts changed how you feel about it?

- If you can, tell it again, and make it as light as you can.

Remember the definition: spiritual ZEST is the influence, connection, and communication that you have to your higher self. It is manifested in activities that heal, renew, comfort, inspire, and lift you up. The ZESTERS help you do that.

CHAPTER 19
SPIRITUAL/SENSUAL CONNECTION

Awakening and manifesting spiritual ZEST heightens and brightens the connection and relationship that you have with your higher self. My higher self, my authentic self, must have been very lonely at times because I forgot all about communicating with her. Now, when I look back, I can see that those were very dark and bleak times for me on my earthly journey.

Opening your heart is a spiritual act that opens you to love. Remember the first time you fell in love with another sentient being? It might have been the puppy or kitten that you had, the aunt from out of town who you adored, or the teenage swoon you felt for someone in high school. It was like being in a movie; every sense in your body was on high alert. Love awakens the five major human senses at quantum speed.

Although researchers may be debating how many human senses exist, everyone agrees that there are at least five senses: sight, hearing, taste, touch, and smell. Through the higher vibration of love, the roses that your lover delivers with a sweet whisper (hearing) and a kiss (taste) are more beautiful, colorful (sight), fragrant (smell), and soft (touch).

Dr. Bruce Lipton, PhD, in "A Love Bomb Interview Excerpt—On Living in Love Versus Fear for Health" said: "When people are in love, they express tremendous vitality. But when people are in fear and in protection, the life force seems to be drained out of them. Basically, nature is really trying to tell us to move toward this higher vibration of love."

Your first love and most profound, lasting, never ending love must be for yourself. Falling in love is a spiritual act that opens your heart. Being in the state of love is being in a state of grace. There is no turning back; your heart is open. Let your love flow and become one with all love. Love for yourself raises your vibration and makes you a magnetic, attractive being.

Feel the radiance of love that comes from deep within you and let it heal the world. You are worthy of being loved and now you must love. Love is your greatest connection to your higher self and it is irresistible.

Where and how you are in your life is because you set that intent five years ago. Conscious intent is created with both spiritual and sensual ZEST. If you did not set a conscious intent for your life, then your unconscious set the intent for you based on your behavior patterns that followed your beliefs. Where and how you are in your life is because of all the moments that have come before. Everything follows what precedes. Everything comes from something. Everything follows what was pre-seeded.

Understanding the connection between spiritual and sensual ZEST prepares you to accept the pivotal role that they have in manifesting your dreams and desires and your ideal life. You may already be living spiritual/sensual ZEST and you are not even conscious of it. That's great. You have it because you are spiritual ZEST. Your higher self provides you with truth and knowledge when you need it; it is your guardian, the voice of reason within you. The more you listen to it, the more the negative, sassy voices in your head quiet down.

CHAPTER 20
ALIGN YOUR FEELINGS AND BELIEFS

"If you have ZEST and enthusiasm,
you attract ZEST and enthusiasm.
Life does give back in kind."
—*Norman Vincent Peale*

Every life has a reason to be here on Earth at this time. We all have our own paths to follow, stories to live, and bundles to carry. When you attract more ZEST and enthusiasm you have more gifts to share with the world. So much of life is not tangible; you can't touch it, but you can feel it. Too much energy is misused and wasted on fear, anger, and gossip. It is up to us, as responsible humans, to maximize the positive effects of our ZEST, and we can do it with a minimum of expended energy.

"Just sheer life cannot be said to have a purpose because look at all the different purposes it has all over the place. But each incarnation, you might say, has a potentiality, and the mission of life is to live that potentiality. How do you do it?' My answer is, 'Follow your bliss.' There's something inside you that knows when you're in the center, that knows when you're on the beam or off the beam. And if you get off the beam to earn money, you've lost your life. And if you stay in the center and don't get any money, you still have your bliss."
—*Joseph Campbell*

Satisfaction, Frustration, and Desires

The floodgates of ZEST, love, and enthusiasm burst open when we let them flow and open our hearts with pure intent for the lives we want to live. The following five questions help clarify the direction you desire for your life. Write down your answers and the date. Take a breath, go deep inside, and relax. Let's get started.

Clarification

1. Find the feelings of satisfaction, appreciation, and gratitude in your life?

   - What satisfies you most about your life?

   - What do you appreciate most in your life?

   - What are you most grateful for in your life?

   - What are the sources of your satisfaction, appreciation, and gratitude?

2. What frustrates you most about your life are the barriers that hold you?

   - Where in your life do you have the most frustration?

   - Where in your life do you have the least amount of satisfaction?

   - Who frustrates you? Is it your job, your relationships, your boss, your family, your friends, your "situation"?

   - Does it frustrate you that you are living your life aligned with someone else's vision of what your life *should* look like?

   - Is there a gap between where you are and where you want to be or where you think you *should be*? The "should be" is important because you may be trying to align your life to someone else's vision, values, and expectations.

3. What do you need to double your happiness this year?

- Can you do more of what brings you satisfaction?
- What strategies to improve your life have you tried that didn't work?

4. What strategies have you tried to improve your life that have worked?

- Have you read books, taken courses, or joined groups?
- Do you need real, practical actions that you can implement and practice on a daily basis? The more you know about yourself, the more you choose the right actions for your life.

5. What are you trying to accomplish this year?

- What are your personal challenges for the next year?
- Are you willing to narrow that gap between the life that you *are* living and the life that you *want* to be living?

The answers to these questions help eliminate your frustrations and the strategies that haven't worked. They also clarify your desires and reveal strategies that have worked. Your dreams and desires manifest when they are aligned with your values. The next chapter explores your values so that you can take action and live a life that *you* create and care about.

Affirmation:
I am fulfilled, complete, and powerful
in living my life my way.

CHAPTER 21
VALUES: MAPS THAT GUIDE YOU

"Values are people's most important life priorities, the bases for what they actually do, what they want to accomplish, and how they want to be. When we live out our values, we commit our actions to the important matters of our lives, not the trivial. Ideas like 'individual character' are built around deeply held values, and the meanings and world views associated with them."

—*Paul H. Ray*

Values change to reflect the culture and society of the day. Public perception of smoking and its acceptance has changed. For years, smoking was accepted anywhere and anytime; that has changed because societal values have changed. Not drinking and driving is a value that has changed. Years ago, the general population didn't think twice about having several alcoholic drinks and then driving home. Wearing a seat belt and wearing a helmet to ride a bike or motorcycle are values that are now commonplace.

For example, a big fraud case in the United States revolved around the CEO at WorldCom. He probably didn't set out to commit fraud. He juggled the books a bit to save people's jobs and make more money for the shareholders. However, he juggled the books and the whole thing came down and caused a financial crisis. The CEO may tell you that honesty was one of his values, but when it was tested his actions didn't align. So obviously this was not one of his values.

When you get together with friends and family you may imitate the behaviors that you saw when you were younger. You may do the same things that you saw your mother and aunts doing: laughing, cooking, working. Were they having fun? Values are similar. We tend to mimic what we see, unless we are given reason to question those actions or values and realign with new ones.

Where and when do values start? Even before kindergarten, you learned some values from your image makers. They are the people in your life who mold and sculpt you into the person they want you to be. In 1988, Robert Fulghum published the following poem about values.

ALL I REALLY NEED TO KNOW I LEARNED IN KINDERGARTEN

All I really need to know about how to live and what to do and how to be I learned in kindergarten. Wisdom was not at the top of the graduate-school mountain, but there in the sandpile at Sunday School. These are the things I learned:

Share everything.

Play fair.

Don't hit people.

Put things back where you found them.

Clean up your own mess.

Don't take things that aren't yours.

Say you're sorry when you hurt somebody.

Wash your hands before you eat.

Flush.

Warm cookies and cold milk are good for you.

Live a balanced life—learn some and think some

and draw and paint and sing and dance and play

and work every day some.

Take a nap every afternoon.

When you go out into the world, watch out for traffic,

hold hands and stick together.

Be aware of wonder.

CLARIFY AND PRIORITIZE YOUR CURRENT VALUES—PART ONE

Knowing your values and living them makes you the Goddess of your own life and dreams. It gives you the ZEST to uncover your authentic self and stop trying to become something you are not. This means you'll stop feeling frustrated with yourself. The absence of frustration is the perfect soil for real growth, passion, and ZEST.

I had a client who said she wanted to go work for an NGO (non-governmental organization) in Africa. She was very frustrated that the courses she took turned out to be useless and she could not get any traction toward this dream. She did the values exercise and discovered that "family" was her number one value. She had two children, an eight year old and an eighteen month old.

Among her top values were *family, adventure,* and *advancement.* She realized that she had to be aligned with her values and to make her dreams come true she needed to find meaningful work that would allow her to raise her family. It wasn't long before she landed a job that gave her *adventure and advancement.* It had great benefits, a good working environment, and a pay scale that far exceeded what she would have made working for an NGO; plus she was able to work from home and book her appointments around her family.

I had another client who had recently been recruited into a new, exciting, high paying job, but she was having difficulty getting along with her teenage daughter. Her top values included *success, prosperity, and challenge.* Nowhere did she mention family! In an instant, she knew that her focus had not been in the right place and she changed her mindset. She had been so busy providing for her three daughters that she had forgotten how important they were to her. Her job turned out not to be the dream job that she had been promised. She now has found a work and family balance that is aligned with her values.

Take only seven to ten minutes to sort your values and don't over think it. There are more than 130 values listed, but don't hesitate to add to the list. Don't get hung up on the definition of the words; apply your own meaning and understanding.

Create five column headings across the top of a page in this order:

Always valued	Often valued	Sometimes valued	Seldom valued	Least valued

Read over the values and list the ones that resonate to you so that you have ten in each column. Then arrange the columns from the top down, most important to least important.

You also have the option of downloading these as values cards from www.ZESTyourLife.com/extras. You can print them, cut them out, and sort them. The above "header cards" are included in the download.

When you are finished, your top values will be in the "always valued" column, descending in order of importance to you. Make a note of your five top values.

Take another look at the values that you have remaining and make note of your five lowest values.

Remember that values change, so it may be fun to take a picture of your values for today and date it.

Acceptance	Competence	Exploration	Leadership	Rationality
Accomplishment	Competition	Faith	Learning	Recognition
Achievement	Connectedness	Fairness	Listening	Resiliency
Advancement	Consensus	Family	Love	Respect
Adventure	Contributing	Fashion	Loyalty	Responsibility
Affection	Control	Fitness	Moderation	Risk-taking
Appearance	Cooperation	Focus	Movement	Romance
Appreciation	Courageous	Forgiveness	Nature	Security
Artistic expression	Creativity	Freedom	Neatness	Self-acceptance
Attractiveness	Decisiveness	Friendship	Notoriety	Self-esteem
Authority	Dedication	Fun	Nurturing	Self-respect
Awareness	Devotion	Generosity	Organization	Self-control
Autonomy	Dependable	Grace	Originality	Sensitivity
Balance	Discipline	Growth	Passion	Service
Beauty	Diligence	Harmony	Patience	Sharing
Belonging	Diplomacy	Health	Partnership	Spirituality
Boldness	Effectiveness	Helping	Participation	Stability
Caring	Efficiency	Honesty	Peace	Style Solitude
Challenge	Elegance	Humor	Perseverance	Spontaneity
Charisma	Enjoyment	Imagination	Personal develop-ment	Success
Choice	Enthusiasm	Independence	Playfulness	Teamwork
Clarity	Environment	Influence	Pleasure Power	Tolerance
Collaboration	Excellence	Integrity	Process	Tradition
Communication	Excitement	Intellectual status	Prosperity	Tranquility
Community	Expertise	Interdependence	Quality	Trustworthiness
Compassion	Expression	Intimacy	Rationality	Vitality
		Knowledge	Recognition	Wisdom
			Reliability	

Viktor Emil Frankl, M.D., Ph.D. a neurologist and psychiatrist as well as a Holocaust survivor suggests that there are three central values in life:

- The *experiential* is what happens to us in life; who and what we experience, and the love we feel.

- The *creative* is what we bring into existence—music, art, inventions, and projects, including the project of our own lives.

- The *attitudinal*—our responses in difficult circumstances—is what tests our beliefs and values.

Your values give direction and purpose to the way you spend each day. When you feel out of balance, often it's because you are not behaving in a manner that is aligned with your values. Perhaps you say your spouse, partner, or children are the most important things to you in the world; are you behaving in a manner that aligns with that? If they are the most important value in your life, are you nurturing your relationship with them? How do you express that value in your life?

If making ZEST in your life is a value, then what are you doing to make that happen? What actions are you taking every day? What ZESTERS are you using? *Choosing to live the life you want, aligned with your values, becomes the legacy you leave.*

VALUES IN ACTION—PART TWO

For each of your top five values, write a specific example of how you express that value in your life. If you find that you have values that are not expressed in your life, you will want to spend some quality time to reconcile your values with the life you are living. For example, if you value adventure, but you never go anywhere or do anything, how can you manifest this you value into your life?

The bottom five values are also important to know. When you are setting your intent for your life, if any of them are aligned with your bottom five values, then you are unlikely to get that wish or to feel fulfilled if you do. What this means is, if travel to South America is on your list, but the value of "adventure" is in the bottom five values, there's a disconnect. Your mind and intent do not align to make adventure travel manifest in your life. It can't happen—the energy required to manifest into your reality is absent because of the gap between your values and your wishes. *Your values should always lead the way.* How are your bottom values present in your life?

If you do something against your values, then the result could be disastrous. When did you do something that you really didn't want to do? Something that you knew was wrong and opposite to your values? What was the result?

If you are working with others on this exercise, discuss with them their top values and their bottom values; they are the most significant. Were there any surprises in part one of this exercise? In a work environment, knowing if someone values creativity or tradition helps to give assignments and tasks to the appropriate people. It also can explain why you are attracted to certain tasks and you resist others.

In a *Success Magazine* interview, Howard Schultz, CEO of Starbucks, was talking about how the company "Reclaimed Its Mojo". He said, "I think one of the most vital things that came out of our transformation was the confidence we gained knowing we could preserve our values despite the internal and external challenges we faced...It is easy to abandon ideals when a ship is sinking and just row. But our values steadied us when our stock, our reputation, and our performance were all at their lowest points."

> *"...Values are not luxuries for prosperous times.*
> *They are necessities in all times."*
> —*Howard Schultz*

Wow, I liked Starbucks before…

Affirmation:
I know my values and live my life aligned with my values.

You now know:

- What your values are.

- How values are expressed in your life.

Values must be aligned with every decision you make or you won't be living your authentic life. You know that you are not aligned with your values when you are trying to make a decision and you keep changing your mind from day to day and even moment to moment. You may have a physical reaction, an uncomfortable feeling, or a headache. *Trust your values.*

CHAPTER 22
FREEDOM

*"Intuition is an energy pocket that opens so that
you know what to do."*
—Lisa LaJoie, Spiritual Teacher

Time and time again, both women and men choose *freedom* as their highest value. History clearly shows that human kind, animals, and all sentient beings go to great lengths to gain freedom.

To have the life you want, to be your authentic self, and to follow your life path, you must have freedom. To have freedom, you must claim your freedom and that's what *ZEST Your Life* is about—vibrant freedom. It means that you have the prowess and capability to live your genuine destiny. The Freedom Wheel that I developed relates ZEST in the emotional, physical, mental, spiritual, and core aspects. The Freedom Wheel sets you *free* to have a spirited, dynamic, and actualized life. You need your personal freedom to live your heart's desire and your values.

Start at the bottom of the wheel; what would be south if this was a compass. This is the emotional aspect—the freedom to feel and be fully aware of the emotions circulating in everyone who is involved. Understand and perceive the significance, explanation, or cause of the circumstances and appreciate and recognize the full worth of a situation in emotional balance. Balanced, emotional ZEST in high measure gives you the freedom to choose your attitude and approach. You are not psychologically affected by the behavior of others. It is *emotional maturity*. Can you remember when or even if you felt emotional ZEST power in high measure?

On the left side of the wheel look at the physical aspect—the freedom to create the representation of the external form; plan the course of action and let it manifest in the physical reality. With the freedom to create and a plan, you can now manifest into tangible, physical reality. Everything humans have made came to be in this way.

At the top, your mind has the freedom to think; discern, perceive, recognize, judge, evaluate, and decide to come to a resolution as a result of considering your beliefs with mental clarity. This is the freedom to judge and decide what you believe and what you want in your life because what you believe is what you have in your life. This is where you set your intentions; if you don't, someone else's beliefs will rule your life.

On the right, your spiritual aspect is manifested in the freedom to find; discover and honor, implement and fulfill your divine purpose in life. It is trusting your higher self, your intuition, and your values.

Orgasmic freedom is the passion to openly and honestly express your authentic life force energy. It involves taking the lid off of your energy and showing your beauty, gifts, and talents to the world. It is the center - the core - that drives and makes all the directions possible. This is the catalyst that holds all the power and energy of the emotional, physical, mental, spiritual, and orgasmic aspects together and enables you to *ZEST Your Life!*

Having freedom takes courage. You cannot have freedom without courage. Life is too short to not be living your heart's desire.

CHAPTER 23
YOUR AUTHENTIC SELF

You know your values and you have your freedom. Now let's look at how you are going to gain further clarity to live your life from the heart. Your heart's desire is not found in your head; it's in your heart and how you feel. Your feelings form the compass that guides you to stay true to the direction of your heart's desires and to fulfill your dreams.

BE WHO YOU REALLY ARE

You will want to make note of your answers.

1. Who are you? Describe your qualities and personality traits in a list of words—not your roles of daughter, friend, etc. For example, if people describe Oprah, they might say: strong, passionate, persevering, etc. If you have a hard time describing yourself, imagine someone who loves you and knows you well (like your higher self) describing your qualities and personality traits. Here are some suggested words to get you started:

Artistic	Creative	Exacting
Passionate	Enthusiastic	Precise
Entertaining	Provocative	Expectant
Commanding	Energetic	Demanding
Engrossing	Sensual	Sexy
Funny	Fun	ZESTY

2. What do you love? What you love tells the story of who you are and what you're about. Make a list of what you love. Did you put down that you love to whine and complain? I didn't think so. If you don't love it, perhaps you shouldn't do it. That's not always possible, but we have far more choices in life than we allow ourselves.

3. Live your life differently. Would you live differently if you knew you only had one year, six months, or three months left to live? This is not your bucket list of things to do. You may decide to *do* some of the things you have always wanted to do, but the emotionality and mindset you bring into it dictates how you *live* in those moments. I'm suggesting you *live* differently, not *do* differently. Would you have more gratitude and appreciation every moment?

Would you live differently if you knew you had another seventy, eighty, or one hundred years to live? If you would live differently, then I must ask, "If you are not living your life differently now, when will you?"

Henry David Thoreau said, "I wanted to live deep and suck out all the marrow of life..." That's ZESTY!

4. What is your gift, your passion? Why are you here? Explore and live by your why. What do people ask you for advice about? The advice that people seek from you is one of your gifts. Ask for what you can give, not only what you want. Give and you shall receive.

Affirmation:
I am the best of me.

Positive Power Talk

Every day, in the media and maybe from our family and friends, we hear unachievable ideals and negative or debasing messages. The antidote to heal this hurtful input is to replace it with positive talk to ourselves and to others.

If you are doing this exercise alone, look in the mirror and speak the words to your image.

If you are doing this with others, you may want to work in pairs. Take turns and speak the words to the woman at whom you are looking:

- Say, "You are a ZESTY, power-filled woman."

- Everyone defines "ZESTY, power-filled woman" in their own way. Pause, feel it in your body, and take in the words. Notice any feelings that come up, both as you receive the words and as you say the words.

- If you are doing this exercise alone, speak the words again as you look in the mirror. "You are a ZESTY, powerful woman."

- Now, look in her eyes or your own eyes in the mirror, and say, "I am a ZESTY, powerful woman."

Pause and feel it in your body. Can you own it? Can you say these words as an intent statement? "I am a ZESTY, powerful woman?" Practice. Practice every day. Look in the mirror each morning, and say: "I am a ZESTY, powerful woman." Put a note on your mirror to remind yourself. Believe the words as you speak them.

Now, hold your definition of "ZESTY, powerful woman" in your mind. *She is you; she is your higher self. Walk in her footsteps.*

This is important because you are changing an old belief. A belief that no longer serves you. Now you must do what your "ZESTY powerful woman" does. Accept only opportunities and offers that feed and nurture your powerful woman.

Most of us are not good at accepting compliments. Practice *giving* sincere compliments. When we learn to give, we can learn to receive.

Connect to your heart to share what you feel when you are in the presence of a powerful woman. For example, "I see a powerful woman. When I am in your presence, I am filled with warmth. I feel smart and wise."

When someone asks, "How are you?" what is your answer?

"I'm ZESTY!" Everyone wants what you have.

You will inspire them to find their inner ZEST as well.

**Affirmation:
I am a ZESTY woman.**

PASSION POWER
Secret #5 Women with ZEST honor their dreams and desires.

The passion of a dream can never be underestimated. It is manifested from your core life force energy. All of the art—and every piece of music—are all fueled by it. I think of all the women who immigrate to a new country to make better lives for themselves and/or their families. They were motivated by life force energy because they took action.

What is your dream or passion for something you want to do, learn, or accomplish?

What three things do you want to do in your life that you have never done?

1.

2.

3.

Affirmation:

Every day, I am closer to my dreams coming true.

Following are some ways to engage your orgasmic life force energy.

- Wear purple panties. Trust me. You increase your ZEST when you wear purple panties. When you put on purple panties you absolutely know you're going to have a great day. Purple is the color of royalty and I think it's a spiritual and sexual color. I don't know why it works, but I've known this for years and I was surprised how many hits I got when I Googled "purple panties."

- Read erotic literature. Reading erotic literature engages your mind and emotions; your body reacts in a positive way. It may provide you with some great new ideas.

- Kiss. According to Helen Fisher, PhD, in *Why Him? Why Her? How to Find and Keep Lasting Love,* "Kissing stimulates all the senses. When you kiss you see your partner, as well as smell, taste, hear, and feel him or her. The lips have a huge number of sensory neurons that pick up the slightest messages. Then cranial nerves escort these myriad sensations to the brain where they are processed in the somatosensory cortex. This impressive factory of the senses picks up signals from all around the body. But the vast majority of this brain region is devoted to processing sensations from around the nose and mouth, which gives your lips and tongue their exquisite sensitivity.

And kissing affects more than just your senses. It boosts your pulse and blood pressure, dilates your pupils, and deepens breathing. In men, kissing even raises levels of oxytocin, the neurochemical associated with trust and attachment. And in both sexes, kissing reduces the stress hormone, cortisol. So kissing bombards the brain, bringing pleasure and relaxation.

It also gives you vital information about what your partner has been eating, drinking, and smoking. So as we kiss, we are assessing the habits, health, immune system, chemistry, and intention of a potential mate.

Both men and women say that kissing brings them emotionally closer to their partner—at least a good kiss does. Tender, passionate, considerate: people tend to reason that a sensitive kisser will be a suitable partner, spouse, and co-parent."

- Share hugs. Change your language from "giving a hug" to "sharing a hug." You can feel the ZEST, right?

Neurophysiologist Jürgen Sandkühler, head of the Centre for Brain Research at the Medical University of Vienna, points out that hugging someone can help reduce stress, fear, and anxiety. It has a lowering effect on blood pressure, promotes well being, and improves memory performance. These positive effects are caused by the secretion of the peptide oxytocin.

Oxytocin, a hormone produced by the pituitary gland, is primarily known for increasing bonding, social behavior, and closeness between parents, children, and couples. Increased oxytocin levels have been found in partners in functional relationships. In women, it is also produced during the childbirth process and breastfeeding in order to increase the mother's bond with the baby.

"The positive effect only occurs, however, if the people trust each other, if the associated feelings are present mutually, and if the corresponding signals are sent out," adds Sandkühler.

The same applies to the length of the hug. "Hugging is good, but no matter how long or how often someone hugs, it is trust that's more important." Once the trust is there, positive effects on the oxytocin level can be achieved simply as a result of the increased emphatic behavior, says the brain researcher. "Studies have shown that children whose mothers have been given extra oxytocin have higher levels of the hormone themselves, i.e. solely as a result of the mother's behavior."

- Rejuvenate your spirits in a physical way. If you are with someone and you have mutual agreement, share a hug now. Getting, giving, or sharing hugs with strangers is not recommended and could have negative, stressful effects.

- Increase your pleasure. Making love, pleasure, and guiltless self-pleasuring increase your life force energy that fuses your ZEST. Making love is the ultimate joining of energy with another person. Some people believe that it ties your energy to the other person for seven years. Be very discerning and share this special, spiritual time only with those in whom you share absolute respect and trust. Spiritually, orgasm transcends and shifts your energy to a different mindset. Physically, it releases endorphins that make you feel great and improve your health. It is good for the emotions, the mind, and the body.

"One of the lovely areas of love where space can be rendered beautiful is when two people make love. The one you love is the one to whom you can bring the full array and possibility and delight of your senses in the knowledge that they will be received in welcome and tenderness. Since the body is in the soul, the body is illuminated all around with soul-light. It is suffused with a gentle, sacred light. Making love with someone should not be merely a physical or mechanical release. It should engage the spiritual depth that awakens when you enter the soul of another person."
—*John O'Donohue*

- Are you taking care of your sensuality and your sexuality? Do you know what you like and want? Is there passion in your lovemaking, even if you are not with a partner? Living your authentic life and being your authentic self is so important that I have used the word authentic more than fifty times. It takes trust in yourself to appreciate your true, reliable, dependable, honest, real, valid, rightful, legitimate self. It's who you really are. Your authentic self is strong, but fragile. You nurture and reinforce it by honoring who you really are by using only positive self talk and digging deep into your passion power.

CHAPTER 24
CREATE A ZEST VISION BOARD

A vision board is a physical display of your values, dreams, and desires. It is a tool to help you clarify, visualize, and focus on the life you want. Creating a vision board sends a message to the universe that you intend to attract all this goodness into your life. It is the Law of Attraction in action.

The one thing that blocks the Law of Attraction is negative energy. So clear away any guilt, fear, and anger; these emotions are all rooted in the past. Step your life into the present and implement all those behaviors that we discussed previously.

At the end of this chapter, you will have:

- An accountability partner.

- A written list of what you want in your life.

- A clearly identified vision of the life you want.

- A tool to keep you focused on your dreams and desires.

- A way to measure your progress as you see your images manifest in your life.

Think about what you want your life to be. Once you know what you want, ask for it. Be specific and trust that you are going to get what is best for you and your higher self. Don't be concerned that you have a life of abundance and you want more. Humans are made to want more; otherwise, we would all still be riding tricycles and would be satisfied with that.

A Dominican University of California study shows that when you write down your wishes, dreams, and what you want in your life, you have a 76 percent better chance of making them come true. Dr. Gail Matthews states, "My study provides empirical evidence for the effectiveness of three coaching tools: accountability, commitment, and writing."

1.   Find an accountability partner. This is someone who you want to work with to do this exercise. You keep this person responsible for following every step of this exercise and your partner helps you do the same.

2.   Make a list of at least fifty wishes, dreams, and desires you want in your life. Making a list stimulates the super consciousness and seeds what you intend to birth. Tip: you may list a certain dollar amount, but also ask for what that money would buy.

Don't think too much about any one item on the list; just keep listing what comes to mind. You need at least fifty items before you start thinking of the "whacky wishes." For most people, the first ten or twenty are easy and then they think they're done. Don't give up. Keep writing and you may be surprised when you include wild and crazy stuff simply to finish the list. It may turn out that your "whacky wishes" are the dreams and desires that have been hiding in your subconscious.

Get a clear vision of the life you want and explore your dreams and desires in each energetic aspect of yourself. If your list exceeds fifty, that's okay too. You want to make sure that you have as complete a list as possible.

Have a drink of water, get comfortable, and take a deep breath in and out. Now explore each manifestation of energy.

Emotional energy—How do you want to feel consistently or occasionally? Do you want calm, peace, excitement, adventure, and more? When you are clear on that feeling, can you describe it? If it is new and not on your list already, be sure to write it down. Take a deep breath in and out.

Physical energy—What do you want your body to be like? How about the house, the car, the money, or anything that you touch? When you are clear, can you describe how you want each one to be? If it is new and not on your list already, write it down. Take a deep breath in and out.

Mental energy—How would you describe your ideal mental and intellectual capacity? What provides you with the mental stimulation you seek? When you are clear, can you describe it? If it is new and not on your list already, add it now. Take a deep breath in and out.

Spiritual energy—Do you want a connection to your higher self, the greater power, God or Goddess? How do you want that to manifest and what is that relationship to be? When you are clear, can you describe it? If it is new and not on your list already, write it down. Take a deep breath in and out.

Sexual/catalyst energy—Do you want to combine all of the above to create a vibrant, exciting life? When you are clear, can you describe your life in each aspect? Again, if it is new, include it now. Then take a deep breath; in and out.

We have been talking a great deal about you, your desires, your dreams, and what lights you up. I have one last question: *How are you going to make the world a better place?* When you are clear, can you describe your life in each aspect? If you can think of something new, write it down.

3. Check your list. The list should include items that bring you joy and ZEST in the emotional, physical, mental, spiritual, and orgasmic aspects. Imagine the feeling you have when each one of these is manifested in your life. Major categories that you want to address:

Health	Career	Friends
Family	Love	Travel
Prosperity	Relationships	Knowledge
Wealth	Partner	Education
Success	Creativity	Learning

4. Turn your vision board into a collage. Equipment required is: foam board, magazines, pictures, tape, and scissors. I recommend foam board because it sits up straight and doesn't flop over like construction paper. I like 20 by 30 inches or 51 by 77 cm. It's available at dollar stores for under two dollars. I prefer to use tape instead of glue so that it is easy to move and change the images without destroying them. Choose magazine cuttings that reflect your personal interests and things on your list. Oprah Magazine is excellent because it has quotes and sayings that are illustrated in attractive fonts.

5. Get some pictures that illustrate your dreams and desires. Cut out pictures, quotes, and sayings that are meaningful to you and evoke the feelings you want to have. As you are looking for pictures that are on your list, you may come across something that was not on your list; add it now. Include a picture of yourself in your vision board. There are several ways you can lay out your vision board:

- Organize your images according to each aspect: emotional, physical, mental, spiritual, and sexual/catalyst.

- Organize it in categories: relationships, career, health, wealth and prosperity, lifestyle, creativity, self development, travel, adventure, etc.

- Organize your dreams and desires according to the Freedom Wheel (review it again by flipping back to Chapter Twenty-Two).

6. Take action to bring yourself closer to your dreams and desires. Making a list is a good start, but showing the commitment and initiative to get the ball rolling increases the positive energy to make it manifest. Share your vision board with someone who cares and can help you be accountable to do at least one thing each day that brings you closer to your dreams and desires.

7. Date your list. When you review your list in six months or a year, you are able to check off all the items you have received. I prefer not to cross them out, instead I put a check beside them so I can still see them. You may want to start a "success journal" for all of your accomplishment and dreams that come true.

8. Put your ZEST Vision Board under your bed and dream with it for seven nights. Take a good look at it before you go to sleep, breathe in and out a few times, picture your vision in your mind, and dream it into reality.

9. Place your Vision Board in a prominent place where you will see it every single day. Take a good look at it and connect with the energy of your desires every day. Review and revise it regularly as your dreams come to fruition and to ensure that it remains an accurate reflection of your desires in all areas of your life. I recom-

mend redoing your Vision Board at least once a year near your birthday. It's a nice way to reflect on the progress you have made and where you want to go.

Congratulations! You have accomplished a great deal to get yourself closer to living your authentic life and manifesting your dreams and desires.

You have:

- An accountability partner.

- A written list of what you want in your life.

- A clearly identified vision of the life you want.

- A tool to keep you focused on your dreams and desires.

- A way to measure your progress as you see your images manifest in your life.

CHAPTER 25
TESTS AND CHALLENGES

"It is only when we're falling apart that we know what holds us."

—*Chameli Ardagh*

You may be challenged and tested with situations that require great strength and power. We are never tested on our strengths, only our weaknesses. Every time life falls apart we heal, grow, and transform it into a stronger and more authentic life. You read these words, but you do not know that you have ZEST in all your aspects (emotional, mental, physical, spiritual, and catalyst) until you are tested. And trust me, you will be tested.

It is ironic to me that while I was writing this book, what I was writing about fear, anger, emotional maturity, and more all came up and slapped me in the face—not only once, but several times. This gave me the opportunity to put the tools and resources provided into practice and even to develop some new ones.

When you have times that you don't feel your ZEST, you must generate it. I had to admit out loud that I don't always feel ZESTY. Because it doesn't happen very often and dealing with it isn't in my everyday toolbox. I dig deep, search for the real feelings, and am honest with myself—really honest with myself. I check into my emotions, my body, and my mind and connect with my spirit guides.

The answer often is that I had not been taking care of myself. I was "too" busy to be mindful of my emotions, my body, my mind, and my spirit. I was "too" busy to ask for help. Stepping into the truth with gratitude, courage, and kindness to myself shifted my mindset and set me free. My ZESTY, vibrant self was back! Tune into your own ZEST, get to know it intimately, then you will know when to turn it up and when to sit quietly with it.

"The power plant doesn't have energy, it generates energy."
—Brendon Burchard

You don't know how strong you are until you are tested. Go back to your first power story. You didn't know you could face it, do it, solve it, live through it, but you did. You have demolished beliefs and barriers. They are not strangers to you and with your experience you'll dismantle them easily and freely with self-confidence, courage, and no regrets.

"We think our biggest problem is that we're not supposed to have problems. Problems are the gifts that make us dig and figure out who we are and what we're made for. And what we are responsible to give back to life."
—Tony Robbins

When you're going into a difficult situation where you know there will be complainers and difficult people, wear no panties to remind yourself to laugh and not take yourself too seriously.

"Remember—the only taste of success some people have is when they take a bite out of you."
—Zig Ziglar

CATALYST

A catalyst triggers change.

Often it takes a catalyst to make changes in life. Being fired, a relationship breakup, moving to a new city, and/or illness can spark you to review and renew beliefs, gain a new understanding of yourself and how to do what you do, and figure out why you are wired this way.

Shift to a positive mindset and your life moves up a notch or two—or it takes a quantum leap. A catalyst takes you out of inertia and into movement and action. It stimulates your life force energy. As listed in Chapter One, there are *Seven Secrets of Women with ZEST*. Here is **Secret #6 Women with ZEST take action to make a difference.**

If you have a dream of going to the Olympics, you got the idea, "I want to go to the Olympics." The passion to work hard and be the best in your sport is the sexual catalyst energy that gets you there. It is the get up and go that drives you to the next level of performance.

When you surmount obstacles and challenges with beauty and grace without complaining, then you know that you have achieved ZEST. You have created a rainbow from the rain. Your behavior and responses of positive ZEST ripple out to everyone in your family, everyone you meet, and even the people you pass by in the mall or on the street. It is like a stone thrown in a pond; it ripples out seven times and ripples back to you seven times. You may not see your impact, but clear away your doubts and trust that it is happening.

LIVE YOUR ZEST REVIEW

You have reached a new level of understanding about yourself, your relationships, and the world around you. You have created a new image of yourself and what and whom you believe yourself to be. Your mindset has shifted! You software has been upgraded.

Let's review Part 4—Live Your ZEST—and the clarity gained:

- You have an understanding of where you get satisfaction and what frustrates you.

- Your dreams and desires are defined and you have tools to manifest and implement them.

- Your values and how they are expressed in your life are the cornerstones to living your ZEST.

- You have freedom in all aspects.

- You are a ZESTY, power-filled woman and you don't need anyone's permission to say so!

- You now align your wishes with your values to gain the freedom of being your authentic self.

- You have created and activated a ZEST vision board.

CHAPTER 26
PART 4—ZESTERS

How do you manifest ZEST in your life? What do you do with the ZEST that you have? These are the ZESTERS that bring ZEST, emotional maturity, and mind/body balance to every aspect of your life and your relationships in every moment of each day. They set the habit for a powerful, vibrant life. When shit happens in your life—and it will— you turn to these ZESTERS to retune, renew, and reinvigorate you.

- Change your pattern to think in order of: self, life, and others. Put yourself first. Change the pattern of putting others first by teaching them how to take care of themselves. Tough love may be required, but you know in the long run it is for the best.

- Be of service to others only without sacrificing your authentic self.

- Open your heart and enjoy the sensations of energy surges, warmth, and vulnerability that the spiritual experience can trigger.

- Cherish and nurture feeling uplifted and powerful; encourage it in others.

- Listen to spiritual music that will open your heart to love. I like to choose music that doesn't remind me of anything; it has no holds to images or past thoughts. Go to www.ZESTyourLife.com/extras for a link to a free music download.

- Engage in spiritual dancing. Get together with a group of women, put on some tunes, and dance. It's merely dancing, but if you do this a few times it transforms you and you feel the spirit lift.

- Try spiritual walking, running or cycling. Performing a repetitive activity, such as running, can calm the mind while exercising the body. Many walkers, runners and cyclists describe a feeling of peace that is gained when they reach an optimal stride or cadence. This combination of mind/body is spiritual ZEST.

- Live by The Five Agreements (from the books, *The Four Agreements* and *The Fifth Agreement*, by Don Miguel Ruiz). Here is a great tool that you can consider your personal code of conduct. Living by these agreements improves your relationship with your higher self and with others and increases your spiritual ZEST.

The Five Agreements by Don Miguel Ruiz:

1. Be impeccable with your words. Speak with integrity. Say only what you mean. Avoid using the word to speak against yourself or to gossip about others. Use the power of your word in the direction of truth and love.

2. Don't take anything personally. Nothing others do is because of you. What others say and do is a projection of their own reality, their own dream. When you are immune to the opinions and actions of others, you won't be the victim of needless suffering.

3. Don't make assumptions. Find the courage to ask questions and to express what you really want. Communicate with others as clearly as you can to avoid misunderstandings, sadness, and drama. With just this one agreement, you can completely transform your life.

4. Always do your best. Your best is going to change from moment to moment; it will be different when you are tired as

opposed to well rested. Under any circumstance, simply do your best and you will avoid self-judgment, self-abuse, and regret.

5. Be skeptical, but learn to listen. Don't believe yourself or anybody else. Use the power of doubt to question everything you hear. Is it really the truth? Listen to the intent behind the words and you will understand the real message.

• Explore Animal Totems. Draw understanding of yourself and others from animal totems. You are probably familiar with sun sign astrology that connects a particular zodiac sign to where the sun was on your date of birth. Sun Bear developed *The Medicine Wheel: Earth Astrology*, which relates an animal totem to your date of birth.

Date Range	Zodiac sign:	Earth Astrology Animal Totem:
Dec 22–Jan 19	Capricorn	Snow goose
Jan 20–Feb 18	Aquarius	Otter
Feb 19–Mar 20	Pisces	Cougar
Mar 21–Apr 19	Aries	Red hawk
Apr 20–May 20	Taurus	Beaver
May 21–Jun 20	Gemini	Deer
Jun 21–Jul 22	Cancer	Flicker
Jul 23–Aug 22	Leo	Sturgeon
Aug 23–Sep 22	Virgo	Brown bear
Sep 23–Oct 23	Libra	Raven
Oct 24–Nov 21	Scorpio	Snake
Nov 22–Dec 21	Sagittarius	Elk

Find your animal totem; get to know and understand the characteristics, living conditions, and behaviors of your animal totem and what it means to you. Imagine yourself as your totem animal and notice how it changes your perspective.

Study the animal totems of the people closest to you. Learn to understand their characteristics and how they can interact with you and your own animal totem's characteristics. Imagine them as their totem animal; notice how it changes your perspective.

For example, the beaver is hardworking; family is of prime importance and a beaver values home and hearth. This means that a person with a beaver totem probably wants to stay in the same home and keep it comfortable and constant. They are happiest when they entertain their family and friends in their homes as opposed to going out.

The more you understand what motivates and inspires you and those around you, the more peace you experience. You stop trying to change others and accept them for who they are and you see and accept your own magnificent self.

Affirmation:
Every day, I understand and
love myself more and more.

- Start or visit a spiritual garden. How does an acorn become a mighty oak? It is believed by many that plants and trees hold magic. Plants and trees have always been used for their medicinal and spiritual power; that's where modern medications came from. There was great meaning to the expression of the sixties, "flower power." It meant love, peace, and freedom. Even if you can't plant a garden, taking a moment to observe and feel the energy of plants and trees can be a soothing balm to the mind, body, and soul.

- Take a break, walk outside, and recite the Beauty Way Prayer to reestablish beauty in your life and connect you to your higher self.

After you come inside, ask yourself what being outside did for your spirit? Being outside is a great way to reconnect with your spiritual higher self, realign your life, renew all your senses, and balance your male and female energies. Use it as a screen saver on your computer; go to www.ZESTyourLife.

BLESSED BEAUTY WAY PRAYER

Great Spirit, may I walk in Beauty!

So that I may be a part of the Greater Beauty.

Great Spirit, may I walk in Beauty.

May Beauty be to the left of me,

That I may receive Beauty through my inner woman.

Great Spirit may I walk in Beauty.

May Beauty be to the right of me,

That I may give Beauty through my inner man.

Great Spirit, may I walk in Beauty.

May Beauty be behind me,

So that the only tracks I leave are those of Beauty.

Great Spirit, may I walk in Beauty.

May I touch myself, my Life, and all the others with Beauty.

May I walk this Blessed Beauty Way.

Great Spirit, may I walk in Beauty.

That is what I ask. This is what I will do.

- Sit under a tree, and rest your back firmly into the trunk. Ask that you be shown and given your soul's work for this lifetime. Ask for your spiritual gifts to be shown to you. Sit in silence for twenty minutes with your eyes closed. Give thanks to the Tree Spirits. Pay attention over the next few days and discover why you are here on Mother Earth at this time and at this moment. You have created a direct link to your purpose and how you can fulfill it in this lifetime, one step at a time.

> **Affirmation:**
> **I am guided to bring beauty and love in all that**
> **I say and in all that I do.**

- Take responsibility. The responsibility for the situations you create in your life is yours. Accepting responsibility gives you the power to change your life; otherwise, you project the responsibility onto something or someone else. That is giving away your power.

- Feed your mind. How is your life so far? Good? Okay? Bad? Do you want that answer to be different in ten years, five years, one year, three months, today? Create yourself and your power with every emotion, thought, body sensation, and spiritual and sensual experience—real or imagined.

- Protect your mind. Who are the five people with whom you spend the most time? You become their combined average in income, health, and relationships. Find people who are doing better in the areas you want to improve. Be generous with people who want to reach out to you.

*"In everyone's life, at some time, our inner fire goes out.
It is then burst into flame by an encounter with another
human being.
We should all be thankful for those people who rekindle the
inner spirit."*
—Albert Schweitzer

- Practice gratitude. Be grateful for what you have, for the love and beauty that is your life, and for the opportunities for growth that are put before you—sometimes manifested as challenges.

- Show faith.

*"When you come to the edge of all the light that you know and
you're about to step into the darkness of the unknown, faith is
knowing one of two things will happen for you. There will be
something solid to stand on or you will be taught to fly."*
—Elizabeth Kubler-Ross

- Be brave. Do the challenging and the difficult and you feel your ZESTY Powerful Woman in action. Not everyone can encourage and support the changes in you and your life, but when you know they are right for you, make the changes anyway.

*"Don't be afraid to take a big step. You can't cross
a chasm in two small jumps."*
—David Lloyd George

- Don't give your power away. Instead, give your love away to others. Never accept other people's power, even if they try to give it to you.

- BE. Be and others will see. This is your mission in life. Enjoy life and be happy. What is your purpose? To be joyful and show your joy and ZEST to others. When you heal yourself, you heal your family; when you heal your family, you heal the world.

Enable yourself, your children, and your friends to create a culture of love and to support each other in exploring and applying love, strength, and ZEST for the greater good.

CHAPTER 27
WHY NOW?

"We are visitors on this planet. We are here for one hundred years at the very most.

During that period, we must try to do something good, something useful, with our lives.

If you contribute to other people's happiness, you will find the true meaning of life."

—The Dalai Lama

Why is it important and vital that you should live your ZEST now of all times? Perhaps I should ask you:

Why not now?

If not now, when?

If not you, who?

What are you waiting for?

Will you be living your ZEST in ten years? Yes!

In five years? Yes!

In three years? Yes!

In one year? Yes?

This year?

Yes. Now is the time to dust off your dreams, projects, ideas, and adventures.

> *"Women are the most underutilized economic asset*
> *in the world's economy."*
> —*Angel Gurria, Secretary-General, Organisation for Economic*
> *Co-operation and Development (OECD)*

There is compelling evidence that women can be powerful drivers of economic growth. Our own estimates indicate that raising female employment to male levels could have a direct impact on GDP of 5 percent in the United States, 9 percent in Japan, 12 percent in the United Arab Emirates, and 34 percent in Egypt; but, greater involvement from women has an impact beyond what their numbers would suggest. For example, women are more likely than men to invest a large proportion of their household income in the education of their children. As those children grow up, their improved status becomes a positive social and economic factor in their society. Thus, even small increases in the opportunities available to women, and some release of the cultural and political constraints that hold them back, can lead to dramatic economic and social benefits (from "Empowering the Third Billion Women and the World of Work in 2012," Leading Research).

It's the Best Time to Be a Woman!

According to Astrid Pregel, B.A., MBA, President of Feminomics Inc. www.Feminomics.org

Women are the key to global economic prosperity. In 2015, women are the world's highest educated resource. In every country, except Sub Saharan Africa and two countries in

South Asia, women are the majority of university graduates; this includes every country in the Middle East and Northern Africa.

Women represent over 40 percent of the world's formal labor force. In addition women are the vast majority of the globe's informal workers whether as micro business owners in the informal economy, as unpaid domestic workers, or as caregivers of family and community. If women's work caring for the next generation of global laborers was measured, we find that the value of women's contribution would nearly double global GNP.

Around the world, women invest significantly more of their resources in their families than do men. When women earn income or have some control of family resources, education, nutrition, and health improves and children thrive.

Women drive global and national economies through their importance as consumers. In the USA and Canada consumption represents 71 percent and 51 percent of GNP with women making 90 percent of consumption decisions. The buying decisions of women is more important to the North American economy than the oil and gas, service sector, and the manufacturing industries combined. In fact, the world's women, not including India and China and Brazil, is the fastest growing market in the world. Women's purchasing power will increase from 13 trillion US dollars to 20 trillion US dollars in the next five years.

LOVE YOUR LIFE

When you introduce new energies into your life, you may feel some resistance. That's perfectly normal. Take a deep breath, acknowledge the resistance, and remind yourself of the benefits of the new energies and action. Your focus on yourself and what you want dissolves the resistance. You may want to schedule rereading *ZEST Your Life* into your calendar. It takes time and reinforcement to create new habits and establish new thought processes.

Creating and maintaining ZEST in your life is a process and a journey. Prepare for the unexpected by practicing and honing your skills. Practice your ZESTERS. Daily practice increases your ZEST. Review your ZEST affirmations to focus and program your mindset. Download free ZEST affirmations at www.ZESTyourLife.com/extras. The more ZEST you have, the more ZEST you see in others.

You are a victorious, wisdom warrior. You have a genius, a guide, and a guru inside of you that is a bountiful source of inner knowing and is far more trustworthy than the conscious mind. You hold knowledge about love and what you know about it can be taught to others by the life you live. You make a difference by who you are and the values and virtues you put into the world around you. You are a ZESTY, power-filled woman and you don't need anyone's permission or approval to be who you are.

I believe that you find your own ZEST. What that feels like and looks like—how it affects you, your family, and the world around you—is all up to you. You are recreating your life in a way that touches you and others with love, grace, and beauty. When you contribute to one person's happiness you are changing the world. Your contribution provides growth, expansion, and change. It clarifies your values, tests your emotional maturity, stretches your mind/body into new territory. **Secret #7 Women with ZEST love their lives.**

This is how you rewrite your story and reclaim your powerful ZEST. You have felt the strength, power, and energy in your stories. You already own your ZEST; you're awakening it and taking it back. True power is uplifting, radiating from the inner light deep inside of you. Being a powerful woman means you embody a combination of wisdom and focus that together give you strength and positive feelings. It is not about you fitting in, conforming, and belonging to a social and cultural "norm". It is an exploration and expansion of your freedom, autonomy, and individuality. It flows freely and easily, contributes to the greater good, and enables others to have power. Powerful ZEST is power-filled ZEST.

YOUR ACT OF POWER

"Your act of power is the key to your destiny. Like a sacred flute player enticing your truth of spirit out into the light of day, own your power, because you are made of power. An act of power comes from a place of passion within your deepest being. It is an expression of your totality, of who you are in the world. To find your act of power is to live your dreams. What would you do if you could do anything? Discover what that is, and then do it. To find your power is to find your destiny."

—*Lynn V. Andrews*

What is your act of power? How will you put your authentic self into action? It takes an act of power to find your authentic self, your power-filled, powerful woman. She is the woman you really are. You lead from the road that you have already walked and what your eyes have already seen. The threads of your experiences are pulled together to form the tapestry of your life; make it a beautiful one. Your act of power is waiting for you to take action. Do it now. Your personal story is about leadership, so that you leave a legacy that others can follow. You are an inspiration to others - a magnetic, attractive energy - when you ZEST your life.

"When all these pieces come together, not only does your work move toward greatness, but so does your life. For, in the end, it is impossible to have a great life unless it is a meaningful life. And it is very difficult to have a meaningful life without meaningful work. Perhaps, then, you might gain that rare tranquility that comes from knowing that you've had a hand increasing something of intrinsic excellence that makes a contribution. Indeed, you might even gain that deepest of all satisfactions: knowing that your short time here on this Earth has been well spent, and that it mattered."

—Jim Collins

Congratulations, you have ZEST in your life! We have been on this journey together. Feel the ZEST in every cell of your body and in the spaces between them. ZEST is a way of engaging in life. It's an attitude and it's there for all of us. You are expanded, evolved, and engaged in continuous ZEST and growth. Keep your ZEST alive, active, and healthy by connecting with other ZESTY women on the ZEST Your Life Facebook group: www.Facebook.com/groups/zestyourlife.

Keep in touch at www.ZESTyourLife.com for my blog and information about the new products that I am developing for you.

Give your life, your dreams, and your desires your full and undivided attention. Have fun. If it's not fun, it's not sustainable. When they all come true, make new dreams and help others achieve ZEST in their life.

There is no better time to be succeZESTful!

About the Author

Linda Babulic is *that* woman… the guest you want to sit next to at a dinner party, the speaker who captures your attention, the coach who tailors your solution and makes it all about you, just when it matters most.

From one-on-one consults, to workshops, keynote speeches and books, Linda addresses our growing need for connection and validation. Her flagship "ZEST" program promotes and serves anyone seeking greater meaning, deeper understanding and the kind of joy that comes from the heart. Linda describes living a truly zesty life as Zeroing-in (on your dreams), Expecting (to receive all you deserve), achieving Success (as you define it), and Transcending (to your higher self).

Linda is genuine and enjoys seeing people learn something new and exceed their own expectations. She has spent over 30 years helping people to awaken, develop and actualize their inner wisdom, so that they can create the life they really want and live in the ZEST zone.

Recommended Resources

These books and others are accessible through www.ZESTyourLife.com/extras

Amen, Dr. Daniel. *Change Your Brain Change Your Life*

Andrews, Lynn V. *Medicine Woman* (and all other books)

Bennett-Goleman, Tara. *Emotional Alchemy*

Bolen, Jean Shinoda, MD. *Goddesses in Every Woman*

Borysenko, Joan. *A Woman's Journey to God*

Bridges, Carol. *The Medicine Woman Inner Guidebook*

Chopra, Dr. Deepak. *Ageless Body Timeless Mind* (and all other books)

Covey, Stephen R. *The 7 Habits of Highly Effective People*

Gilbert, Elizabeth. *Eat, Pray, Love*

Hay, Louise. *You Can Heal Your Life affirmations*

McGowan, Kathleen. *The Book of Love*

Nelson, Dr. Miriam E. *Strong Women Stay Young*

Ruiz, Don Miguel. *The Four Agreements and The Fifth Agreement*

O'Donohue, John. *Anam Cara*

Schulz, Mona Lisa, MD, PhD. *Awakening Intuition*

Shapiro, Debbie. *The BodyMind Workbook*

Steward, Laura. *What Would a Wise Woman Do?*

Sun Bear. *The Medicine Wheel: Earth Astrology*

Vitale, Dr. Joe. *Zero Limits: The Secret Hawaiian System for Wealth, Health, Peace, and More*

Weil, Andrew MD. *Spontaneous Healing*

Wieder, Marcia. *Finding Your Dream*

Williamson, Marianne. *A Return to Love*

REFERENCES

Ronald B. Adler and Neil Towne, *Looking Out/Looking In* (New York: Harcourt College Pub, 1998).

Dr. Daniel Amen, *Change Your Brain, Change Your Life* (New York: Harmony, 1999) 105.

Lynn V. Andrews, *The Power Deck* (New York: Tarcher, 2004).

Lynn V. Andrews, *The Woman of Wyrrd: The Arousal of the Inner Fire* (New York: HarperCollins, 1990).

Tara Bennett-Goleman, *Emotional Alchemy* (New York: Harmony, 2001) 210.

Joan Borysenko, *A Woman's Journey to God* (New York: Riverhead Hardcover, 1999) 2, 122.

Carol Bridges, *The Medicine Woman Inner Guidebook* (Stamford, CT: US Games Systems,1991) 181.

H. Jackson Brown, Jr., *Life's Little Instruction Book: Simple Wisdom and a Little Humor for Living a Happy and Rewarding Life* (Nashville: Thomas Nelson 2012) 13.

Leo Buscaglia, *Love: What Life Is All About* (New York: Ballantine Books, 1996).

Joseph Campbell, *The Power of Myth* (New York: Anchor, 1991) 286.

Nick Cannon, *Success Magazine*, November 2012, 15.

Dr. Silvia Helena Cardoso, "What Is Mind?" http://www.cerebro-mente.org.br/n04/editori4_i.htm, accessed May 4, 2015.

Michael A. Cohn, Lahnna I. Catalino, Tanya Vacharkulksemsuk, Sara B. Algoe, Mary Brantley, Barbara L. Fredrickson, "How Positive Emotions Build Physical Health: Perceived Positive Social Connections Account for the Upward Spiral Between Positive Emotions and Vagal Tone" Psychological Science, July 7, 2012, http://www.psychologicalscience.org/index.php/news/releases/social-connections-drive-the-upward-spiral-of-positive-emotions-and-health.html, abstract accessed May 4, 2015.

Jim Collins, *Good to Great* (New York: Harper Business, 2001) 210.

Dr. Stephen R. Covey, *The Seven Habits of Highly Effective People* (New York: Simon & Schuster, 2013).

Harry Crews, *The Scar Love*r (New York: Touchstone, 1993) 142.

Brian L. Davis, Lowell W. Hellervik, James L. Sheard, *Successful Manager's Handbook* (Minneapolis: Personnel Decisions Intl, 1996).

Bert Decker, *The Art of Communicating* (Menlo Park: Crisp Publications, 1997) 96.

Peter H. Diamandis and Steven Kotler, *Abundance: The Future Is Better than You Think* (Florence, MA: Free Press, 2014) 15.

Roger A. Drake, *Familiarity-and-Liking Relationship Under Conditions of Induced Lateral Orientation.* International Journal of Neuroscience 23 (1984): 195-198.

T. S. Eliot, *The Cocktail Party* (New York: Mariner Books, 1964).

Masuro Emoto, *Messages from Water* (New York: Atria Books, 2005).

Helen Fisher, PhD, *Why Him? Why Her? How to Find and Keep Lasting Love* (New York: Holt Paperbacks, 2010).

Elizabeth Gilbert, *Eat, Pray, Love* (New York: Penguin, 2006), 260.

Bruce Lipton, PhD, in "A Love Bomb Interview Excerpt—On Living in Love Versus Fear for Health" https://www.youtube.com/watch?v=bG-ZmecpT8iY, accessed May 4, 2015.

Dr. Gail Matthews, http://www.dominican.edu/dominicannews/dominican-research-cited-in-forbes-article, accessed May 4, 2015.

Kathleen McGowan, *The Book of Love* (New York: Touchstone, 2010).

Dr. Miriam E. Nelson, *Strong Women Stay Young* (Mass Market Paperback, 1997).

John O'Donohue, *Anam Cara* (New York: Harper Perennial,1998) 7.

Cheryl A. Picard, *Mediating Interpersonal and Small Group Conflict* (Toronto: Dundurn, 2002) 68.

Paul H. Ray, PhD, "The Potential for a New, Emerging Culture in the U.S.: Report on the 2008 American Values Survey" www.wisdomuniversity.org/CCsReport2008SurveyV3.pdf, accessed May 4, 2015.

Ranier Maria Rilke, Rilke's Book of Hours: Love Poems to God (New York: Riverhead Trade, 1997) page 88.

Don Miguel Ruiz, *The Fifth Agreement* (San Rafael, CA: Amber Allen Publishing, 2011).

Don Miguel Ruiz, *The Four Agreements* (San Rafael, CA: Amber Allen Publishing, 1997).

Jürgen Sandkühler, Head of the Centre for Brain Research at the Medical University of Vienna http://medicalxpress.com/news/2013-01-good.html, accessed May 4, 2015.

Mona Lisa Schulz, MD, PhD, *Awakening Intuition* (New York: Harmony, 1999) 19.

Sun Bear and Wabun Wind, *The Medicine Wheel: Earth Astrology* (New York: Simon & Schuster Ltd, 1980).

Claire Sylvia, *A Change of Heart* (New York: Grand Central Publishing, 2009).

Neale Donald Walsch, *The Complete Conversations with God* (New York: Penguin, 2005).

Neale Donald Walsch, *The Mother of Invention* (New York: Hay House, 2012) 225.

Dr. Joe Vitale, *Zero Limits: The Secret Hawaiian System for Wealth, Health, Peace, and More* (Wiley, 2008).

Andrew Weil, MD, *Spontaneous Healing* (New York: Ballantine, 2000).

Marcia Wieder, *Finding Your Dream* (On the Mark Branding, 2005)

Marianne Williamson, *A Return to Love* (New York: Harper One, 1996).

Canadian Mental Health Association, http://www.cmha.ca, accessed May 4, 2015.

Harvard Public Health, http://www.hsph.harvard.edu/news/magazine/happiness-stress-heart-disease, accessed May 4, 2015.

Natural Resources Canada. http://www.nrcan.gc.ca/mining-materials/diamonds/industry/8163, accessed May 4, 2015.

CPSIA information can be obtained
at www.ICGtesting.com
Printed in the USA
LVOW01s1209230217
525177LV00001B/3/P